Leveled
Text-Dependent
Question
Stems

Author
Melissa Edmonds, Ed.D.

SHELL EDUCATION

Consultant

Teresa L. Keener
Marsteller Middle School
Bristow, VA

Contributing Author

Jodene Lynn Smith, M.A.

Publishing Credits

Corinne Burton, M.A.Ed., *President*; Conni Medina, M.A.Ed., *Managing Editor*; Emily R. Smith, M.A.Ed., *Content Director*; Lee Aucoin, *Senior Graphic Designer*; Lynette Ordoñez, *Editor*; Stephanie Bernard, *Assistant Editor*

Image Credits

p.73 U.S. National Oceanic and Atmospheric Administration; all other images iStock and/or Shutterstock.

Standards

© Copyright 2010. National Governors Association Center for Best Practices and Council of Chief State School Officers. All right reserved.

© 2007 Board of Regents of the University of Wisconsin System. World-Class Instructional Design and Assessment (WIDA)

Shell Education

A division of Teacher Created Materials
5301 Oceanus Drive
Huntington Beach, CA 92649-1030
www.tcmpub.com/shell-education
ISBN 978-1-4258-1645-2
© 2017 Shell Educational Publishing, Inc.

Table of Contents

What Are Text-Dependent Questions?

From literary novels and dramas, to textbooks, word problems, newspaper articles, scientific reports, primary sources, and websites, texts vary in content and style. Regardless of the format, students must be able to decode and comprehend the contents of the texts to learn from the material. Text-dependent questions (TDQs) increase students' understanding through in-depth examinations of particular aspects of the texts. They guide students to examine specific portions of the texts and then provide evidence for their answers. Unlike other types of questions, TDQs rely solely on the text so that students may not necessarily need to access significant background knowledge or include outside information.

TDQs facilitate the comprehension of text on a variety of levels. On the most specific level, these questions help students analyze words and sentences within the text to determine the specific meanings and connotations of particular words and phrases. TDQs also enable students to study broader concepts, such as text structure and point of view. They aid students in their study of the individuals, settings, and sequences of events in a text and provide a means for investigating the presence of other types of media within the writing (e.g., drawings, illustrations, graphs, tables). These questions offer an effective tool for helping students analyze the overarching themes, concepts, arguments, and claims presented in texts. TDQs help students build their abilities to compare multiple texts to each other on a variety of topics. Through thoughtful design and sequencing, TDQs can be tailored to meet many specific educational standards and learning objectives while still maintaining a direct connection to the text.

Leveled Text-Dependent Questions

Leveling TDQs helps teachers differentiate content to allow all students access to the concepts being explored. While the TDQ stems are written at a variety of levels, each level remains strong in focusing on the content and vocabulary presented in the texts. Teachers can focus on the same content standard or objective for the whole class, but individual students can access the texts at their independent instructional levels rather than at their frustration levels.

Teachers can also use the TDQs as scaffolds for teaching students. At the beginning of the year, students at the lowest reading levels may need focused teacher guidance as they respond to the questions. As the year progresses, teachers can begin giving students multiple levels of the same questions to aid them in improving their comprehension independently. By scaffolding the content in this way, teachers can support students as they move up through the thinking levels.

What Are Text-Dependent Questions? *(cont.)*

Creating TDQs

This book offers 480 text-dependent question stems that can be used to increase reading comprehension in science. Each question stem can be slightly altered to ask the type of question you need. However, it may be necessary to create other TDQs to supplement or support the ones supplied in this book.

When considering what type of TDQ to ask, it is important to think about the key ideas in the text and the desired outcomes of the lesson. What should students understand at the end of the lesson? What are the core scientific concepts of the text? Once these main ideas and objectives have been identified, teachers can determine the particular aspects of the text that should be studied for students to reach these goals. Examine key vocabulary words and important text structures that are related to the underlying core concepts, and develop questions that highlight these connections. Furthermore, identify complex sections of the text that may prove difficult for students, and create questions that allow students to address and master the comprehension challenges presented by the text.

It is also important to consider the sequence of the TDQs presented to students. Generally, the opening questions should be straightforward, giving students the opportunity to become familiar with the text and removing any technical obstacles, such as challenging scientific vocabulary words, which could hinder comprehension. After students gain a basic understanding of the text, introduce more complex questions that strive to illuminate the finer, more intricate concepts. By scaffolding the questions to move from basic, concrete topics to elaborate, implied concepts, you can use TDQs to guide students to a detailed understanding of the complexities of a text.

The key to making sure that questions are dependent on the text is to think about the answer. Can the answer be found in the text, or is an inference created based on facts in the text? If the answer is anchored to the text in some way, it is a strong TDQ!

Setting the Stage for Text Analysis

When using questioning strategies for text analysis, it is vital to establish a safe and collaborative classroom environment. TDQs are designed to stimulate critical-thinking skills and increase reading comprehension in all content areas. It is building these skills, not getting the "right answer," that is the ultimate goal, and students may need to be reminded of this fact. Many TDQs are open ended and don't have single, correct answers. To ensure a collaborative classroom environment, students need to be confident that their answers to questions and their contributions to classroom discussions will be respected by everyone in the room.

TDQs Across the Content Areas

It is usually regarded as the task of the English or language arts teacher to guide students through the effective use of comprehension strategies as they read. Although students read in almost every subject area they study, some teachers may overlook the need to guide students through comprehension tasks with textbooks, analyses of experiments or nonfiction pieces. Comprehension strategies best serve students when they are employed across the curricula and in the context of their actual learning. It is only then that students can independently use the strategies successfully while reading. Students will spend the majority of their adulthoods reading nonfiction expository writing. With this in mind, teachers at all levels must actively pursue ways to enhance their students' abilities to understand reading material. Utilizing TDQs specific to scientific content is one way to achieve this goal.

TDQs can be used to facilitate the comprehension and understanding of any type of text. These strategies can, and should, be applied to any type of text across disciplines and content areas. For example, descriptions of complex scientific concepts, scientific journal articles, or descriptions of experiments provide excellent opportunities for the use of TDQs in the science classroom. Biographies and autobiographies of scientists offer ample opportunities for in-depth study through TDQs as well.

Twenty-First Century Literacy Demands

The literacy demands of the twenty-first century are tremendous. Literacy was defined a century ago by one's ability to write his or her own name. In the 1940s, one needed to be able to read at the eighth-grade level to function adequately in the factory setting. To be considered literate today, one needs to be able to read text written at high school levels as a part of workplace and civic duties and leisure activities.

Students and teachers today have entered a new era in education—one that is deeply tied to the technological advances that permeate the modern world. Today, some children can use cell phones to take pictures before they learn to talk. Students in school use the Internet and online libraries to access information from remote locations. Now more than ever, it is the content-area teacher's responsibility to prepare students for the diverse and rigorous reading demands of our technological age. To become effective and efficient readers, students must utilize comprehension strategies automatically and independently. Students need teacher guidance to help them become independent readers and learners so that they not only understand what they read but also question it and explore beyond it.

TDQs Across the Content Areas *(cont.)*

Integrating Literacy and Science

The goal of literacy in science is to develop students' curiosity about the world around them and promote a knowledgeable population in an ever-changing technological world. Studying the natural world helps students understand how and why things work. Another important goal of literacy in science is to introduce students to the idea of looking at the world and current issues through a critical and scientific lens—to think like a scientist! To accomplish these goals, students must learn how to question, explore, and analyze natural phenomena. With these skills well in hand, students can understand the complexity of available information, are empowered to become independent learners, and learn to consider data that they might otherwise overlook.

Literacy and STEAM Education

STEAM education is a powerful approach to learning that is gaining momentum across the nation. As with many education initiatives, STEAM means different things to different people. Most educators agree that STEAM is the integration of science, technology, engineering, the arts, and mathematics to design solutions for real-world problems. Literacy is an integral part of successfully completing STEAM activities in your classroom. The application of STEAM practices in the classroom affords teachers the opportunity to challenge students to apply new knowledge, often learned through analyzing texts and conducting hands-on activities.

STEAM is a tool educators can use to help students become technologically, scientifically, and mathematically literate. Students engaged in STEAM activities are able to develop important twenty-first century skills: creativity, collaboration, critical thinking, and communication. Students who become STEAM proficient are prepared to answer complex questions, investigate global issues, and develop solutions for real-world challenges. STEAM is a strong component of a balanced instructional approach to ensure that students are college and career ready.

Note
Throughout this book, the term *text* is used in the leveled text-dependent question stems to refer to informational texts, textbook pieces, articles, experiment steps, and so on. When presenting the questions to students, teachers should substitute the specific type of text for that word. The examples illustrate how to do this.

Skills and Descriptions

Literacy-Based Skill	Description	Page
Understanding Scientific Concepts	Students have basic understandings of the scientific concepts in a text to support deeper analysis.	10
Identifying Key Details	Students identify key details that are relevant to the topic and scientific context.	22
Summarizing	Students use the most relevant information to summarize the concepts presented in a text.	34
Using Text Features	Students understand and analyze text features to increase their comprehension of a text.	46
Identifying the Author's Purpose or Position	Students analyze a text to identify the author's purpose or position and how it affects the text.	58
Defining Science Vocabulary	Students use a variety of strategies to define scientific vocabulary.	70
Drawing Conclusions	Students draw conclusions about experiments and investigations based on evidence and data presented in a text.	82
Analyzing Text Structures	Students identify and analyze text structures, noting their purposes and how they affect a text's message.	94
Evaluating Scientific Arguments and Reasoning	Students evaluate arguments and reasoning to determine whether the evidence presented by the author supports his or her claims.	106
Developing Ideas or Processes	Students carefully consider explanations of scientific ideas and processes in a text.	118
Comparing and Contrasting Texts	Students identify similarities and differences between content, text structures, purposes, and text features in multiple texts.	130
Making Inferences	Students use science literacy skills to infer information not directly stated in a text.	142

How to Use This Book

Skill Overview—Each skill is defined on the first page of its section. This explains what the skill is and how to introduce it to students.

Complexity—The text-dependent question stems in this book are differentiated to four complexity levels. The levels roughly correlate to four grade ranges as follows:

- ☆ grades K–1
- ○ grades 2–4
- ☐ grades 5–8
- △ grades 9–12

Implementing the Question Stems—The second page of each section contains an example question stem differentiated to all four complexity levels. This is a great way for teachers to see a model of how the leveled text-dependent questions can be used with their students.

Question Stems—Each of the 12 sections includes 10 question stems differentiated to four complexity levels for a total of 480 questions in the book. Along with a chart showing the 10 question stems, each complexity level also includes a leveled passage with sample text-dependent questions.

K–12 Alignment—The final two pages in each section include the leveled text-dependent question stems in one chart. This allows teachers to use these two pages to differentiate the text-dependent questions for their students.

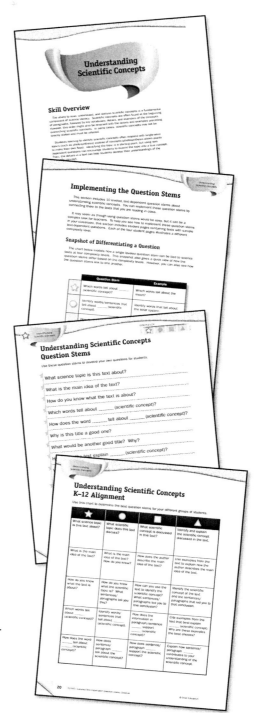

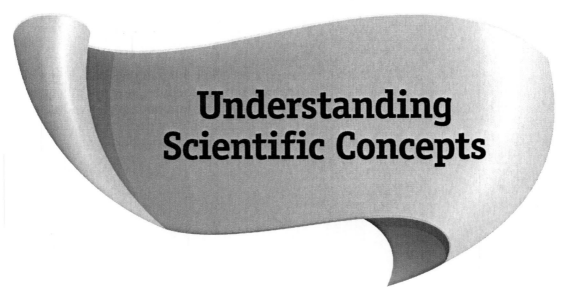

Understanding Scientific Concepts

Skill Overview

The ability to read, understand, and discuss scientific concepts is a fundamental component of science literacy. Scientific concepts are often found at the beginning of paragraphs, followed by key vocabulary, details, and examples of the concepts. However, this order might also be reversed with the details and examples preceding overarching scientific concepts. In some cases, scientific concepts may not be directly stated and must be inferred.

Students learning to identify scientific concepts often respond with single-word topics (such as photosynthesis) instead of concepts (photosynthesis allows plants to make their own food). Identifying the topic is a starting point, but using text-dependent questions can encourage students to expand the topic into a true concept. Then, the details in a text can help students develop their understandings of the scientific concept.

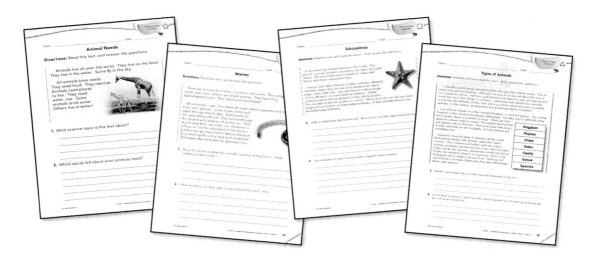

Implementing the Question Stems

This section includes 10 leveled, text-dependent question stems about understanding scientific concepts. You can implement these question stems by connecting them to the texts that you are reading in class.

It may seem as though using question stems would be easy, but it can be a complex task for teachers. To help you see how to implement these question stems in your classroom, this section includes student pages containing texts with sample text-dependent questions. Each of the four student pages illustrates a different complexity level.

Snapshot of Differentiating a Question

The chart below models how a single leveled question stem can be tied to science texts at four complexity levels. This snapshot also gives a quick view of how the question stems differ based on the complexity levels. However, you can also see how the question stems link to one another.

	Question Stem	Example
☆	Which words tell about _____ (*scientific concept*)?	Which words tell about the moon?
○	Identify words/sentences that tell about _____ (*scientific concept*).	Identify words that tell about the solar system.
□	How does the information in paragraph/sentence _____ support _____ (*scientific concept*)?	How does the information in paragraph 2 support what you learned about comets?
△	Cite examples from the text that best explain _____ (*scientific concept*). Why are these examples the best choices?	Cite examples from the text that best explain the Big Bang theory. Why are these examples the best choices?

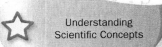

COMPLEXITY

LOW   HIGH

Understanding Scientific Concepts Question Stems

Use these question stems to develop your own questions for students.

What science topic is this text about?

What is the main idea of the text?

How do you know what the text is about?

Which words tell about _____ (*scientific concept*)?

How does the word _____ tell about _____ (*scientific concept*)?

Why is this title a good one?

What would be another good title? Why?

How does the text explain _____ (*scientific concept*)?

What part of the text helps you learn about _____ (*scientific concept*)?

What is the author saying in sentence _____?

Name: _____ Date: _____

Animal Needs

Directions: Read this text, and answer the questions.

Animals live all over the world. They live on the land. They live in the water. Some fly in the sky.

All animals have needs. They need food. They need air. Animals need places to live. They need water, too. Some animals drink water. Others live in water!

1. What science topic is this text about?

_____

_____

_____

_____

2. Which words tell about what animals need?

_____

_____

_____

_____

_____

COMPLEXITY

LOW ★ ○ ■ ▲ HIGH

Understanding Scientific Concepts Question Stems

Use these question stems to develop your own questions for students.

What scientific topic does this text discuss?

What is the main idea of this text? How do you know?

How do you know what the scientific concept is? What sentences/paragraphs tell you this?

Identify words/sentences that tell about _____ (*scientific concept*).

How does sentence/paragraph _____ tell about the scientific concept?

Explain why the title is a good one.

What would be another appropriate title for this text? Why?

How does the author explain _____ (*scientific concept*)?

Which sentence/paragraph helps you best understand the scientific concept?

What scientific concept is described in sentence/paragraph_____?

Name: _____ Date: _____

Worms

Directions: Read this text, and answer the questions.

There are thousands of kinds of worms in the world. They wriggle, creep, and crawl. Worms are simple animals. They have long, tube-shaped bodies. They don't even have brains!

All worms do is eat. They feed off single-celled organisms and waste from other animals. Some ocean worms pull water through their bodies. Earthworms do the same thing with soil. They burrow through the ground and swallow soil as they go. They digest what they can in the soil. Whatever is left passes out the other end of their bodies. Earthworms are important to farmers because they churn up the soil as they burrow and eat. This makes the soil better for growing crops.

1. How do you know what the scientific concept of the text is? What sentences tell you this?

_____

_____

_____

2. What would be another appropriate title for this text? Why?

_____

_____

_____

_____

Understanding Scientific Concepts Question Stems

Use these question stems to develop your own questions for students.

What scientific concept is discussed in this text?

How does the author describe the main idea of the text?

How can you use the text to identify the scientific concept? What sentences/paragraphs led you to this conclusion?

How does the information in paragraph/sentence _____ support _____ (*scientific concept*)?

How does sentence/paragraph _____ support the scientific concept?

Use evidence from the text to explain why the title is appropriate.

Write an alternative title for this text. How is your new title supported by the text?

Use examples to show how the author explain _____ (*scientific concept*).

How do sentences/paragraphs _____ and _____ help you understand the scientific concept?

Explain the scientific concept that is described in sentence/ paragraph _____.

Name: _____ Date: _____

Echinoderms

Directions: Read this text, and study the picture. Then, answer the questions.

Echinoderms are animals that live in the ocean. The phylum, or group, includes sea urchins, sea stars, and sand dollars. The word *echinoderm* is Greek for "spiny skin." That is what most echinoderms have.

Animals have either bilateral or radial symmetry. Bilateral symmetry means that one side of an animal is the mirror image of the other side. Your right hand is a mirror image of your left hand. You have bilateral symmetry. Radial symmetry means that an animal has many identical parts. They are laid out like the spokes on a wheel. All five arms of a sea star are mirror images of one another, so it has radial symmetry. In fact, all echinoderms have five-sided radial symmetry.

1. Write an alternative title for this text. How is your new title supported by the text?

_____

_____

_____

_____

_____

2. Use examples to show how the author explains *radial symmetry*.

_____

_____

_____

_____

_____

Understanding Scientific Concepts
Question Stems

Use these question stems to develop your own questions for students.

Identify and explain the scientific concept discussed in the text.

Use examples from the text to explain how the author describes the main idea of the text.

Identify the scientific concept of the text and the sentences/ paragraphs that led you to that conclusion.

Cite examples from the text that best explain _____ (*scientific concept*). Why are these examples the best choices?

Explain how sentence/paragraph _____ contributes to your understanding of the scientific concept.

Cite evidence from the text to explain how the title supports your understanding of _____ (*scientific concepts*).

Create an alternative title for this text. Explain why your new title is appropriate, using evidence from the text.

Use textual evidence to show how the author explains _____ (*scientific concept*).

Explain how the information in sentences/paragraphs _____ and _____ contribute to your understanding of the scientific concept.

Use details from the text to explain the scientific concept that is described in sentence/paragraph _____.

Name: _____ Date: _____

Types of Animals

Directions: Read this text, and study the chart. Then, answer the questions.

Zoologists used to group animals together because they looked similar. This is called a morphological group. Although it is easy to group animals in this way, it isn't always beneficial. Ostriches and humans both have two legs, but that doesn't mean they have other things in common. Zoologists must identify how animals are similar and different, so they now utilize a system called taxonomy to classify species. In this system, all organisms are divided among five kingdoms.

One of those kingdoms is the Animalia Kingdom, or Animal Kingdom. The Animal Kingdom is then divided into groups called phyla. Animalia has 17 different phyla. For example, there is a phylum for bugs. There are nine phyla for various kinds of worms! The phylum most people are familiar with is Chordata. That is because cats, dogs, lizards, and birds are all chordates. In fact, humans are chordates, too.

Taxonomy keeps dividing; it spreads out like a tree. Each phylum divides into smaller categories called classes. Then, classes are further split into orders. Gorillas, monkeys, and humans are in the order Primates. Orders divide into families, and families divide into genus. Finally, the smallest category is a species. Every living thing goes into a category at each level. Humans fall into Animalia, Chordata, Mammalia, Primates, Hominidae, Homo, and sapiens.

Kingdom
Phylum
Class
Order
Family
Genus
Species

1. Identify and explain the scientific concept discussed in the text.

   _____

   _____

   _____

2. Use textual evidence to show how the author explains why morphological groupings are not always beneficial.

   _____

   _____

   _____

Understanding Scientific Concepts
K–12 Alignment

Use this chart to determine the best question stems for your different groups of students.

★	●	■	▲
What science topic is this text about?	What scientific topic does this text discuss?	What scientific concept is discussed in this text?	Identify and explain the scientific concept discussed in the text.
What is the main idea of the text?	What is the main idea of the text? How do you know?	How does the author describe the main idea of the text?	Use examples from the text to explain how the author describes the main idea of the text.
How do you know what the text is about?	How do you know what the scientific topic is? What sentences/ paragraphs tell you this?	How can you use the text to identify the scientific concept? What sentences/ paragraphs led you to this conclusion?	Identify the scientific concept of the text and the sentences/ paragraphs that led you to that conclusion.
Which words tell about _____ (*scientific concept*)?	Identify words/ sentences that tell about _____ (*scientific concept*).	How does the information in paragraph/sentence _____ support _____ (*scientific concept*)?	Cite examples from the text that best explain _____ (*scientific concept*). Why are these examples the best choices?
How does the word _____ tell about _____ (*scientific concept*)?	How does sentence/ paragraph _____ tell about the scientific concept?	How does sentence/ paragraph _____ support the scientific concept?	Explain how sentence/ paragraph _____ contributes to your understanding of the scientific concept.

Understanding Scientific Concepts
K–12 Alignment (cont.)

★	●	■	▲
Why is this title a good one?	Explain why the title is a good one.	Use evidence from the text to explain why the title is appropriate.	Cite evidence from the text to explain how the title supports your understanding of _____ (scientific concept).
What would be another good title? Why?	What would be another appropriate title for this text? Why?	Write an alternative title for this text. How is your new title supported by the text?	Create an alternative title for this text. Explain why your new title is appropriate, using evidence from the text.
How does the text explain _____ (scientific concept)?	How does the author explain _____ (scientific concept)?	Use examples to show how the author explains _____ (scientific concept).	Use textual evidence to show how the author explains _____ (scientific concept).
What part of the text helps you learn about _____ (scientific concept)?	Which sentence/ paragraph helps you best understand the scientific concept?	How do paragraphs/ sentences _____ and _____ help you understand the scientific concept?	Explain how the information in paragraphs/sentences _____ and _____ contribute to your understanding of the scientific concept.
What is the author saying in sentence _____?	What scientific concept is described in sentence/ paragraph _____?	Explain the scientific concept that is described in sentence/paragraph _____.	Use details from the text to explain the scientific concept that is described in sentence/paragraph _____.

Identifying Key Details

Skill Overview

Key details in science texts are often facts, causes, reasons, and examples. These details are used to support the main ideas of the texts or to help readers strengthen their understandings of scientific concepts. Students can learn to identify key details by answering *who*, *what*, *when*, *where*, *why*, and *how* questions. Transition words and phrases such as *first*, *next*, *for example*, etc. can also indicate key details.

When students have practiced identifying key details, they can then practice thinking like authors. *Why* were those details included? *How* do the key details help us better understand scientific concepts? *What* evidence does the author provide? Answering questions such as these requires students to think critically as they analyze the text. When students understand the purpose of the key details, they can apply this knowledge to their own writing.

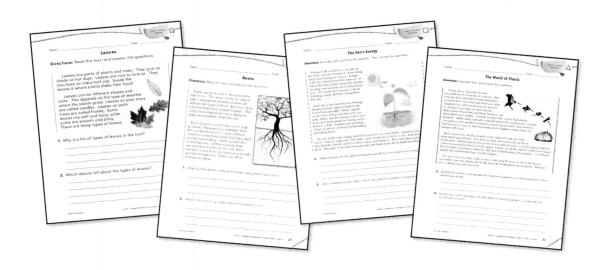

Implementing the Question Stems

This section includes 10 leveled, text-dependent question stems about identifying key details. You can implement these question stems by connecting them to the texts that you are reading in class.

It may seem as though using question stems would be easy, but it can be a complex task for teachers. To help you see how to implement these question stems in your classroom, this section includes student pages containing texts with sample text-dependent questions. Each of the four student pages illustrates a different complexity level.

Snapshot of Differentiating a Question

The chart below models how a single leveled question stem can be tied to science texts at four complexity levels. This snapshot also gives a quick view of how the question stems differ based on the complexity levels. However, you can also see how the question stems link to one another.

	Question Stem	Example
☆	What does the text say about _____ (*scientist*)?	What does the text say about Albert Einstein?
◯	How did _____ (*scientist*) change our understanding of _____ (*scientific concept*)?	How did Isaac Newton change our understanding of gravity?
▢	In what ways did _____'s (*scientist*) discoveries change our understanding of _____ (*scientific concept*)?	In what ways did Marie Curie's discoveries change our understanding of radioactivity?
△	Use details from the text to describe how _____'s (*scientist*) discoveries impacted our understanding of _____ (*scientific concept*).	Use details from the text to describe how Charles Darwin's discoveries impacted our understanding of evolution.

Identifying Key Details Question Stems

Use these question stems to develop your own questions for students.

Which details tell about _____ (*scientific concept*)?

Which details tell about this science topic?

What does the text say about _____ (*scientific concept*)?

What is a key detail in the text?

Why/how does _____ (*event/process*) occur?

What does the text say about _____ (*scientist*)?

How does the text explain _____ (*scientific concept*)?

Why is _____ (*list/example*) in the text?

Why did the author write _____ (*detail*)?

How does the author show that _____ (*scientific concept*) occurs?

Name: _____ Date: _____

Leaves

Directions: Read this text, and answer the questions.

Leaves are parts of plants and trees. They give us shade on hot days. Leaves are nice to look at. They also have an important job. Inside the leaves is where plants make their food!

Leaves can be different shapes and sizes. This depends on the type of weather where the plants grow. Leaves on pine trees are called needles. Leaves on palm trees are called fronds. Some leaves are soft and hairy, while some are smooth and shiny. There are many types of leaves.

1. Why is a list of types of leaves in the text?

_____

_____

_____

_____

2. Which details tell about the types of leaves?

_____

_____

_____

_____

COMPLEXITY

LOW ★ ○ ■ ▲ HIGH

Identifying Key Details Question Stems

Use these question stems to develop your own questions for students.

Which details support _____ (*scientific concept*)?

Which details describe the scientific concept?

What types of details support _____ (*scientific concept*)?

What is the most important detail in paragraph _____?

What reasons/examples are given for why/how _____ (*event/ process*) occurs?

How did _____ (*scientist*) change our understanding of _____ (*scientific concept*)?

How do the details in the text explain _____ (*scientific concept*)?

The author provides a list/examples of _____ (*scientific concept*). What do these have in common?

Why does the author include the details in paragraph/ sentence _____?

How does the author prove _____ (*scientific concept*) occurs?

Name: _____ Date: _____

Roots

Directions: Read this text, and answer the questions.

Plants are anchored to the ground by their roots. This keeps them securely in place during bad weather or when an animal rubs against them. But roots do a lot more than keep a plant in place. The roots' most important role is taking in water and nutrients from the soil.

Roots branch out into the soil to soak up water. The water has nutrients from the soil dissolved in it. Some of these nutrients come from plants that have died and are now rotting. When a plant dies, it decomposes. All the nutrients that are stored in it return to the soil. More nutrients come from decomposing animals and microorganisms. Plants use these nutrients to grow.

1. How do the details in the text explain why plants have roots?

   _____

   _____

   _____

2. What is the most important detail in paragraph two?

   _____

   _____

   _____

Identifying Key Details Question Stems

Use these question stems to develop your own questions for students.

Which details in paragraph _____ support _____ (*scientific concept*)?

Which details does the author use to describe the scientific concept in this text?

What types of details does the author provide to support _____ (*scientific concept*)?

Which detail in paragraph _____ do you think is most important? Why?

What reasons/examples does the text provide for why/how _____ (*events/process*) occur?

In what ways did _____'s (*scientist*) discoveries change our understanding of _____ (*scientific concept*)?

In what ways do the details in paragraph/sentence _____ support _____ (*scientific concept*)?

The author provides a list/examples of _____ (*scientific concept*). How are the items in the list connected?

Which details are most important to understand _____ (*scientific concept*)?

What evidence does the author give to show that _____ (*scientific concept*) occurs?

Name: _____ Date: _____

The Sun's Energy

Directions: Read this text, and study the diagram. Then, answer the questions.

Energy is all around us, every day, all the time—we can't escape it. Every living thing needs energy to survive. Energy is the force that powers the universe—it makes the stars shine, keeps the planets spinning, warms Earth, and makes plants grow. The plants and animals on Earth, including people, get their energy from the sun.

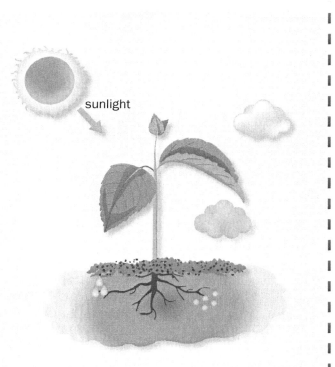

Each day, a massive amount of energy streams through space to Earth in the form of heat and light. Plants capture some of this energy and store it to use later. Plants use this energy to grow and to produce more plants by making seeds, flowers, or fruit. Animals take advantage of this conversion of energy by harvesting and eating plants.

The sun is the main energy source that powers our environment. Heat from the sun causes water to evaporate. The water vapor condenses to form clouds. Rain that falls from the clouds collects in lakes, rivers, and streams. This water allows plants to grow. This cycle is repeated over and over and helps make life on Earth possible.

1. What examples do the text and diagram provide for how a plant uses energy?

   _____

   _____

   _____

2. Which details does the author use to describe the scientific concept in this text?

   _____

   _____

   _____

COMPLEXITY

LOW ★ ● ■ △ HIGH

Identifying Key Details Question Stems

Use these question stems to develop your own questions for students.

Identify the details in paragraph _____ that best support your understanding of _____ (*scientific concept*).

Explain how the author uses details to describe the scientific concept in this text.

Categorize the types of details the author provides to support _____ (*scientific concept*).

Identify the most important scientific detail in each paragraph, and describe the significance of each.

Identify reasons/examples provided in the text that explain why/how _____ (*event/process*) occurs.

Use details from the text to describe how _____'s (*scientist*) discoveries impacted our understanding of _____ (*scientific concept*).

Describe how the details in paragraph/sentence _____ support your understanding of _____ (*scientific concept*).

Describe how the list/examples of _____ (*scientific concept*) in the text supports the main scientific concept.

Identify the details the author provides to support _____ (*scientific concept*). Which details are the most important to understand this concept?

What evidence does the author provide to demonstrate _____ (*scientific concept*) occurs?

Name: _____ Date: _____

The World of Plants

Directions: Read this text, and answer the questions.

Plants are a vital part of many ecosystems for a variety of reasons. Not only are they self-sufficient because they produce their own food, but they have also adapted over millions of years to survive in virtually every type of environment. Many types of animals, including humans, are dependent upon plants. Animals breathe the oxygen that plants produce. Additionally, animals consume plants for sustenance. People consume a wide variety of plants to ensure good health and nutrition. Farmers grow crops in vast amounts, which supplies entire cities of people with food.

Even carnivores, which consume only a diet of meat, are still dependent upon plants. The animals that carnivores eat are likely herbivores. Without plants, the herbivores would not survive, which means that the carnivores would not have a food supply. Plants are at the bottom of the food chain. Even tertiary consumers would be affected if plants were not available. So without plants, the entire food chain would collapse.

The next time you relax under a tree, water your flowers, or sit on the grass, remember how vital plants are to the survival of countless ecosystems. They are even vital to your own survival!

1. Identify the details in paragraph one that best support your understanding of how people use plants.

   _____

   _____

2. Identify the most important scientific detail in each paragraph, and describe the significance of each.

   _____

   _____

   _____

   _____

Identifying Key Details K–12 Alignment

Use this chart to determine the best question stems for your different groups of students.

★	●	■	▲
Which details tell about _____ (scientific concept)?	Which details support _____ (scientific concept)?	Which details in paragraph _____ support _____ (scientific concept)?	Identify the details in paragraph _____ that best support your understanding of _____ (scientific concept).
Which details tell about the science topic?	Which details describe the scientific concept?	Which details does the author use to describe the scientific concept in this text?	Explain how the author uses details to describe the scientific concept in this text.
What does the text say about _____ (scientific concept)?	What types of details support _____ (scientific concept)?	What types of details does the author provide to support _____ (scientific concept)?	Categorize the types of details the author provides to support _____ (scientific concept).
What is a key detail in the text?	What is the most important detail in paragraph _____?	Which detail in paragraph _____ do you think is most important? Why?	Identify the most important scientific detail in each paragraph, and describe the significance of each.
Why/how does _____ (event/process) occur?	What reasons/examples are given for why/how _____ (event/process) occurs?	What reasons/examples does the text provide for why/how _____ (event/process) occurs?	Identify reasons/examples provided in the text that explain why/how _____ (event/process) occurs.

Identifying Key Details K–12 Alignment (cont.)

⭐	⚪	⬛	🔺
What does the text say about _____ (*scientist*)?	How did _____ (*scientist*) change our understanding of _____ (*scientific concept*)?	In what ways did _____'s (*scientist*) discoveries change our understanding of _____ (*scientific concept*)?	Use details from the text to describe how _____'s (*scientist*) discoveries impacted our understanding of _____ (*scientific concept*).
How does the text explain _____ (*scientific concept*)?	How do the details in the text explain _____ (*scientific concept*)?	In what ways do the details in paragraph/sentence _____ support _____ (*scientific concept*)?	Describe how the details in paragraph/sentence _____ support your understanding of _____ (*scientific concept*).
Why is _____ (*list/example*) in the text?	The author provides a list/examples of _____ (*scientific concept*). What do these have in common?	The author provides a list/examples of _____ (*scientific concept*). How are the items in the list connected?	Describe how the list/examples of _____ (*scientific concept*) in the text supports the main scientific concept.
Why did the author write _____ (*detail*)?	Why does the author include the details in paragraph/sentence _____?	Which details are most important to understand _____ (*scientific concept*)?	Identify the details the author provides to support _____ (*scientific concept*). Which details are the most important to understand this concept?
How does the author show that _____ (*scientific concept*) occurs?	How does the author prove _____ (*scientific concept*) occurs?	What evidence does the author give to show that _____ (*scientific concept*) occurs?	What evidence does the author provide to demonstrate _____ (*scientific concept*) occurs?

Summarizing

Skill Overview

Summarizing is a skill that requires students to use both their understandings of the scientific concepts and the key details in a text. They combine these components to create summaries that highlight the most important information in their own words. When students summarize, they demonstrate that they understand the content of a text. In science texts, the sequence in which the information is presented is often important. When students summarize, they should use the same sequence of information.

Younger students may require extra instruction to learn the differences between retelling and summarizing. When students retell, they give as many details as they can remember. When summarizing, students must select only the most important information.

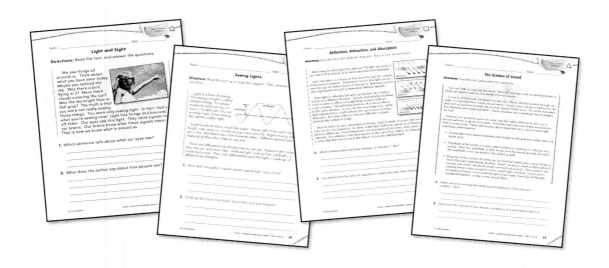

Implementing the Question Stems

This section includes 10 leveled, text-dependent question stems about summarizing. You can implement these question stems by connecting them to the texts that you are reading in class.

It may seem as though using question stems would be easy, but it can be a complex task for teachers. To help you see how to implement these question stems in your classroom, this section includes student pages containing texts with sample text-dependent questions. Each of the four student pages illustrates a different complexity level.

Snapshot of Differentiating a Question

The chart below models how a single leveled question stem can be tied to science texts at four complexity levels. This snapshot also gives a quick view of how the question stems differ based on the complexity levels. However, you can also see how the question stems link to one another.

	Question Stem	Example
☆	What happens first/second/last in _____ (procedure/process/cycle)?	What happens first in a frog's life cycle?
○	List the steps in _____ (procedure/process/cycle).	List the steps in precipitation.
□	Describe each step in _____ (procedure/process/cycle).	Describe each step in the scientific method.
△	Use examples from the text to summarize _____ (procedure/process/cycle) in order.	Use examples from the text to summarize photosynthesis in order.

Summarizing Question Stems

Use these question stems to develop your own questions for students.

What is this text mainly about?

Which sentence tells about _____ (*scientific concept*)?

What is a key fact about _____ (*scientific concept*)?

Which part of the text is the most important?

What does the text say about _____ (*concept/main idea*)?

What happens first/second/last in _____ (*procedure/process/ cycle*)?

Why did the author tell about _____ (*procedure/process/cycle*)?

What did you learn from this text?

What was sentence _____ about?

What does the author say about _____ (*scientific concept/ process*)?

Name: _____ Date: _____

Light and Sight

Directions: Read this text, and answer the questions.

We see things all around us. Think about what you have seen today. Maybe you noticed the sky. Was there a bird flying in it? Were there clouds covering the sun? Was the sky bright blue or dull gray? The truth is that you were not really seeing  those things. You were only seeing light. In fact, that's what you're seeing now! Light hits things and bounces off them. Our eyes see this light. They send signals to our brains. Our brains know what these signals mean. That is how we know what is around us.

1. Which sentence tells about what our eyes see?

_____

_____

_____

2. What does the author say about how people see?

_____

_____

_____

_____

Summarizing Question Stems

Use these question stems to develop your own questions for students.

What did you learn about _____ (*scientific concept*) in this text?

Which sentence best explains _____ (*scientific concept*)?

What are the most important ideas about _____ (*scientific concept*)?

What are the most important ideas/discoveries in this text?

What details support ___ (*concept/main idea*)?

List the steps in _____ (*procedure/process/cycle*).

Why did the author include_____ (*procedure/process/cycle*) in the text.

Which details/facts did you learn from the text?

What is one important idea from paragraph _____?

How does the author explain _____ (*scientific concept/process*)?

Name: _____   Date: _____

Seeing Lights

Directions: Read this text, and study the diagram. Then, answer the questions.

Light is a form of energy. The energy of light is called radiant energy. To radiate means to send out rays or waves. People can only see a certain type of this energy. We call this visible light.

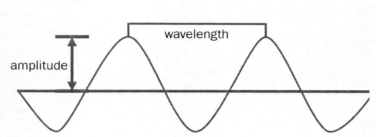

Light travels in waves, much like water. Waves differ from each other in length, rate, and size. Lower-energy waves are red. Higher-energy waves are violet. And there are colors between them. Different wavelengths make up all the colors that we can see.

There are different kinds of light that we can see. Natural light comes from the sun and other stars. Artificial light, such as from lightbulbs, is made by people. They look different because the light is made up of different wavelengths.

1. How does the author explain where natural light comes from?

   _____

   _____

   _____

2. What are the most important ideas in this text and diagram?

   _____

   _____

   _____

Summarizing Question Stems

Use these question stems to develop your own questions for students.

Describe the scientific concept that this text explains.

Which sentence gives the best summary of _____ (*scientific concept*)? Why?

Summarize the concept of _____ (*scientific concept*).

Summarize the most important ideas/discoveries in this text.

Which details best support the concept/main idea in the text?

Describe each step in _____ (*procedure/process/cycle*).

Why did the author include information about _____ (*procedure/ process/cycle*) in this text?

Explain what you learned, using at least three scientific details/ facts from the text.

Use details/facts from the text to explain the main idea of paragraph _____.

Summarize the author's explanation of _____ (*scientific concept/ process*)?

Name: _____ Date: _____

Reflection, Refraction, and Absorption

Directions: Read this text, and study the diagrams. Then, answer the questions.

What happens when light hits objects? The light can bend, it can reflect off a surface, or it can be absorbed into materials.

Light rays bend, or refract, as they travel through the surface of transparent material. *Transparent* means that light can be seen through an object and move through it. Refraction occurs when light travels through a material at different speeds.

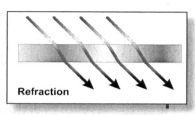

Refraction

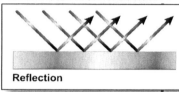

Reflection

When light is reflected, the light rays bounce off a surface and go in a different direction. Smooth and polished surfaces, such as mirrors, reflect more light than surfaces that are rough or bumpy. The light that bounces off a mirror reflects in the same direction, so you can see your image in it. When light reflects from a rough surface, the rays bounce in many directions. It is impossible to see your reflection in paper because the surface is rough.

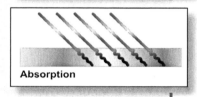

Absorption

When it comes to color, absorption is the key. Light is made of waves, and each color has its own frequency. So when visible light strikes an object, each frequency behaves differently. Some frequencies are absorbed and not seen, while others are reflected. The reflections are what appear as the color of an object. It's important to know that the color is not in the object—it is in the reflected light.

1. Which sentence gives the best summary of reflection? Why?

   _____

   _____

   _____

2. Use details from the text and diagrams to explain the main idea of paragraph two.

   _____

   _____

   _____

Summarizing Question Stems

Use these question stems to develop your own questions for students.

Summarize the scientific concept presented in this text.

Which sentence provides the most succinct summary of _____ (*scientific concept*)? Why?

Summarize the concept of _____ (*scientific concept*) as it is presented in the text.

Summarize and describe the most important ideas/discoveries in this text, and explain why they are significant.

Which details best support the scientific concept/main idea presented in this text? Why?

Use examples from the text to summarize _____ (*procedure/ process/cycle*) in order.

What is the significance of _____ (*procedure/process/cycle*) in this text?

Summarize the text, using at least three scientific details/facts that you learned.

Use scientific details/facts from the text to summarize the main idea of paragraph _____.

Use details from the text to summarize the author's explanation of _____ (*scientific concept/process*).

Name: _____ Date: _____

The Science of Sound

Directions: Read this text, and answer the questions.

Our ears help us navigate the world. Although hearing is not our primary sense, it helps our species survive in a variety of environments.

Sound is created from vibrations of materials. These vibrations pulse through air, water, or solid objects to create sound waves. Sound waves are perceived by the ear and sent as impulses through nerves that connect to the brain. The brain translates the impulses and recognizes them. These impulses are, essentially, the messages we hear.

However, not all sound waves are alike, and the subtle differences allow us to discern between a variety of sounds. Scientists have discovered that sound waves differ in many ways. These differences can be described as a wave's wavelength, amplitude, and frequency.

- Wavelength is the distance between the troughs or the peaks on either side of a single wave.

- Amplitude is the height of a wave, and it relates to loudness or softness of a sound. When the amplitude is high, we perceive the sound as loud, but when the amplitude is low, we perceive the sound as soft.

- Frequency is the number of cycles per second that waves pass a given location, which the brain understands as pitch. Faster vibrations result in higher-pitched sounds, and slower vibrations create lower-pitched sounds. This explains why inhaling helium makes people's voices sound higher pitched. Sound waves produced by human voices pass through helium faster than they do through regular atmosphere, so the voices sound higher.

1. Which sentence provides the most succinct summary of how sound is created? Why?

   _____

   _____

2. Summarize the concept of how sound is created as it is presented in the text.

   _____

   _____

Summarizing K–12 Alignment

Use this chart to determine the best question stems for your different groups of students.

★	●	■	▲
What is this text mainly about?	What did you learn about _____ (*scientific concept*) in this text?	Describe the scientific concept that this text explains.	Summarize the scientific concept presented in this text.
Which sentence tells about _____ (*scientific concept*)?	Which sentence best explains _____ (*scientific concept*)?	Which sentence gives the best summary of _____ (*scientific concept*)? Why?	Which sentence provides the most succinct summary of _____ (*scientific concept*)? Why?
What is a key fact about _____ (*scientific concept*)?	What are the most important ideas about _____ (*scientific concept*)?	Summarize the concept of _____ (*scientific concept*).	Summarize the concept of _____ (*scientific concept*) as it is presented in the text.
Which part of the text is the most important?	What are the most important ideas/ discoveries in this text?	Summarize the most important ideas/ discoveries in this text.	Summarize and describe the most important ideas/ discoveries in this text, and explain why they are significant.
What does the text say about _____ (*concept/main idea*)?	Which details support _____ (*concept/main idea*)?	Which details best support the concept/ main idea in the text?	Which details best support the scientific concept/main idea presented in this text?

Summarizing K–12 Alignment *(cont.)*

★	●	■	▲
What happens first/second/last in _____ (*procedure/process/cycle*)?	List the steps in _____ (*procedure/process/cycle*).	Describe each step in _____ (*procedure/process/cycle*).	Use examples from the text to summarize _____ (*procedure/process/cycle*) in order.
Why did the author tell about _____ (*procedure/process/cycle*)?	Why did the author include _____ (*procedure/process/cycle*) in the text?	Why did the author include information about _____ (*procedure/process/cycle*) in this text?	What is the significance of _____ (*procedure/process/cycle*) in this text?
What did you learn from this text?	Which details/facts did you learn from the text?	Explain what you learned, using at least three scientific details/facts from the text.	Summarize the text, using at least three scientific details/facts that you learned.
What was sentence _____ about?	What is one important idea from paragraph _____?	Use details/facts from the text to explain the main idea of paragraph _____.	Use scientific details/facts from the text to summarize the main idea of paragraph _____.
What does the author say about _____ (*scientific concept/process*)?	How does the author explain _____ (*scientific concept/process*)?	Summarize the author's explanation of _____ (*scientific concept/process*).	Use details from the text to summarize the author's explanation of _____ (*scientific concept/process*).

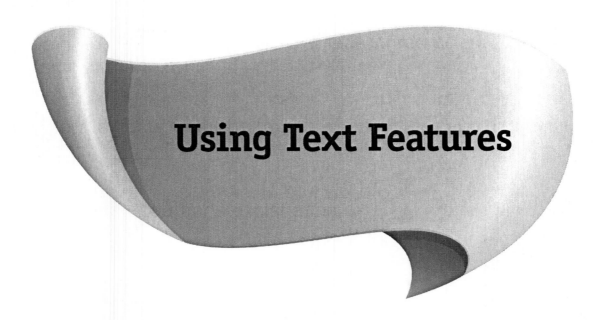

Using Text Features

Skill Overview

Text features are the parts of a text other than the main body text. These features can include headings, bold print, pictures, captions, diagrams, graphs, and charts. These text features can present new information or supplement the body text. However, students are likely to ignore them during reading. Therefore, students must be shown the importance of using text features to increase their comprehension of the text.

Young students who are learning to read are taught to use the pictures to preview texts and make predictions. Older students who are learning to read scientific texts can use text features in the same way. This can help them learn key vocabulary and ideas necessary to understand the scientific concepts presented. Reviewing text features after reading helps students understand why the text features were included and helps them understand how the text features contribute to their understandings of the scientific concepts.

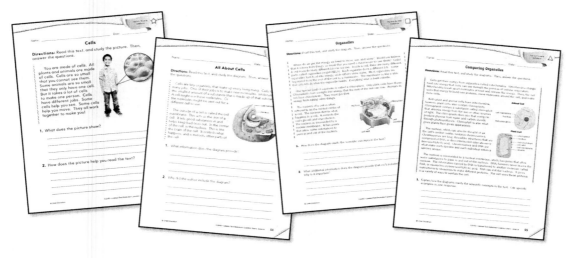

Implementing the Question Stems

This section includes 10 leveled, text-dependent question stems about using text features. You can implement these question stems by connecting them to the texts that you are reading in class.

It may seem as though using question stems would be easy, but it can be a complex task for teachers. To help you see how to implement these question stems in your classroom, this section includes student pages containing texts with sample text-dependent questions. Each of the four student pages illustrates a different complexity level.

Snapshot of Differentiating a Question

The chart below models how a single leveled question stem can be tied to science texts at four complexity levels. This snapshot also gives a quick view of how the question stems differ based on the complexity levels. However, you can also see how the question stems link to one another.

	Question Stem	Example
☆	Look at the chart/graph/image/diagram. What happens first?	Look at the diagram of the ant's life cycle. What happens first?
○	What are the parts/steps of the chart/graph/diagram/image?	What are the parts of the diagram of the flower?
□	What is the order of events for _____ (*scientific process*), according to the chart/graph/diagram/image?	What is the order of events for a tsunami, according to the diagram?
△	Use the chart/graph/diagram/image to summarize the order of events for _____ (*scientific process*).	Use the diagram to summarize the order of events for mitosis.

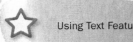

Using Text Features Question Stems

Use these question stems to develop your own questions for students.

What is the title of this text?

What does the heading tell about _____ (*scientific concept*)?

What would be another good heading for this section?

What does the _____ (*text feature*) tell/show?

What does the _____ (*text feature*) tell/show you about _____ (*scientific concept*)?

What does the chart/graph/picture tell about _____ (*scientific concept/main idea*)?

How does the chart/graph/picture help you read the text?

What does the _____ (*text feature*) show that is not in the text?

What does the chart/graph/picture tell about?

Look at the chart/graph/diagram/image. What happens first?

Name: _____ Date: _____

Cells

Directions: Read this text, and study the picture. Then, answer the questions.

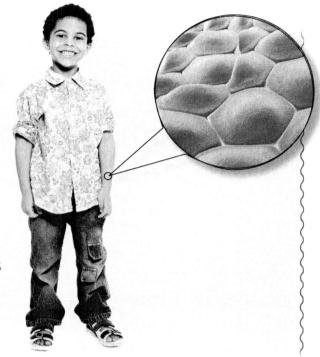

You are made of cells. All plants and animals are made of cells. Cells are so small that you cannot see them. Some animals are so small that they only have one cell. But it takes a lot of cells to make one person. Cells have different jobs. Some cells help you see. Some cells help you move. They all work together to make you!

1. What does the picture show?

_____

_____

_____

_____

2. How does the picture help you read the text?

_____

_____

_____

_____

Using Text Features Question Stems

Use these question stems to develop your own questions for students.

What is the purpose of the title of this text?

How do the headings tell about _____ (*scientific concept*)?

What would be a good subheading for paragraph _____?

Why did the author include _____ (*text feature*)?

What does the _____ (*text feature*) help you understand about _____ (*scientific concept*)?

How does the chart/graph/diagram/image support _____ (*scientific concept/main idea*)?

How does the chart/graph/diagram/image help you understand the scientific ideas in the text?

What does the _____ (*text feature*) show that isn't included in the text?

What information does the chart/graph/diagram/image provide?

What are the parts/steps of the chart/graph/diagram/image?

Name: _____ Date: _____

All About Cells

Directions: Read this text, and study the diagram. Then, answer
the questions.

Cells are tiny organisms that make up every living thing. Cells have
many jobs. One of their jobs is to make new molecules. Molecules are
the smallest amount of a substance that is made up of that substance.
A cell might use these molecules. Or
the molecules might be sent out for a
different cell to use.

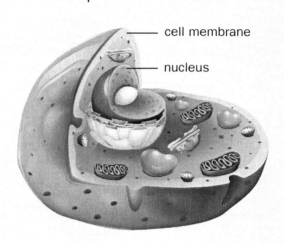

cell membrane

nucleus

The outside of a cell is called the cell
membrane. This acts as the skin of a
cell. It lets good substances in and
helps keep bad ones out. In the center
of the cell, is the nucleus. This is like
the brain of the cell. It controls what
happens, and it instructs other parts of
the cell.

1. What information does the diagram provide?

_____

_____

_____

2. Why did the author include the diagram?

_____

_____

_____

Using Text Features Question Stems

Use these question stems to develop your own questions for students.

How does the title support _____ (*scientific concept*)?

- -

How do the headings and subheadings relate to _____ (*scientific concept*)?

- -

Write a descriptive subheading for paragraph _____. How does it support the text?

- -

How does _____ (*text feature*) support the text?

- -

How does the _____ (*text feature*) support your understanding of _____ (*scientific concept*).

- -

How does the chart/graph/diagram/image support _____ (*scientific concept/main idea*)?

- -

How does the chart/graph/diagram/image clarify the scientific concepts in the text?

- -

What additional information does the _____ (*text feature*) provide that isn't included in the text? Why is it important?

- -

Summarize the information given in the chart/graph/diagram/image.

- -

What is the order of events for _____ (*scientific process*), according to the chart/graph/diagram/image?

Name: _____ Date: _____

Organelles

Directions: Read this text, and study the diagram. Then, answer the questions.

Where do we get the energy we need to move, eat, and sleep? Would you believe that it comes from things so small that you need a microscope to see them? Cells! A cell must do many different jobs to survive. Inside a cell, there are many different parts called organelles (or-guh-NELS). Each organelle does a different job. Some organelles turn food into energy, while others store water. Most organelles are separated from the rest of the cell by a membrane. The membrane is like a skin that only lets in what the organelle needs. Everything else is kept outside.

One special kind of organelle is called a chloroplast. Only plant cells have these. Chloroplasts turn sunlight into energy that the rest of the cell can use. Animals do not have chloroplasts. They must get their energy from eating other things.

The nucleus of a cell is often referred to as the control center of a cell. The nucleus directs what happens in a cell. It controls the cell's growth and reproduction. The nucleus is surrounded by a nuclear membrane. It has pores that allow some substances to pass in and out of the nucleus.

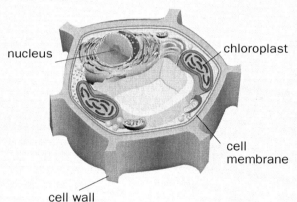

nucleus

chloroplast

cell membrane

cell wall

1. How does the diagram clarify the scientific concepts in the text?

   _____

   _____

   _____

2. What additional information does the diagram provide that isn't included in the text? Why is it important?

   _____

   _____

   _____

Using Text Features Question Stems

Use these question stems to develop your own questions for students.

Explain how the title contributes to your understanding of _____ (*scientific concept*).

Describe how the headings and subheadings are related to _____ (*scientific concept*).

Create a purposeful subheading for paragraph _____, and explain how it supports the text.

How does _____ (*text feature*) support your understanding of the text?

Use examples from the text to explain how the _____ (*text feature*) supports your understanding of _____ (*scientific concept*).

Use examples from the text to describe how the chart/graph/diagram/image supports _____ (*scientific concept/main idea*).

Explain how the chart/graph/diagram/image clarifies the scientific concepts in the text. Cite specific examples in your response.

Analyze any additional information the _____ (*text feature*) provides that isn't included in the text and why it is important to include.

Use key details to summarize the information given in the chart/graph/diagram/image.

Use the chart/graph/diagram/image to summarize the order of events for _____ (*scientific process*).

Name: _____ Date: _____

Comparing Organelles

Directions: Read this text, and study the diagrams. Then, answer the questions.

Cells get their energy from organelles called mitochondria. Mitochondria change food into energy that cells can use through the process of cellular respiration. Mitochondria break apart molecules of food and release the energy. Then, the cell uses that energy to build new proteins, move molecules around the cell, and make more cells.

Both plant and animal cells have mitochondria; however, plant cells also contain chloroplasts. Chloroplasts contain a substance called chlorophyll that absorbs energy from the sun or other sources of light. The chloroplasts then use that energy to produce glucose from water and carbon dioxide through photosynthesis. Chlorophyll is also what gives plants their green appearance.

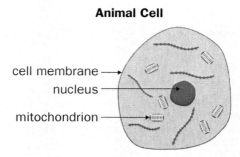

The nucleus, which can also be thought of as the cell's control center, contains chromosomes. Chromosomes are long, threadlike structures that are composed of DNA, or deoxyribonucleic (dee-ahx-ee-ry-bow-noo-KLAY-ik) acid. Chromosomes and DNA are what make each species and each individual within a species unique.

The nucleus is surrounded by a nuclear membrane, which has pores that allow some substances to pass in and out of the nucleus. DNA, however, never leaves the nucleus. The information carried by DNA is transferred to another molecule called RNA, or ribonucleic (ry-bow-noo-KLAY-ik) acid. RNA can exit the nucleus. It gives instructions to ribosomes to make different proteins. The cell uses these proteins in a variety of ways to sustain the cell.

1. Explain how the diagrams clarify the scientific concepts in the text. Cite specific examples in your response.

_____

_____

_____

_____

Using Text Features K–12 Alignment

Use this chart to determine the best question stems for your different groups of students.

★	●	■	▲
What is the title of this text?	What is the purpose of the title of this text?	How does the title support _____ (*scientific concept*)?	Explain how the title contributes to your understanding of _____ (*scientific concept*).
What does the heading tell about _____ (*scientific concept*)?	How do the headings tell about _____ (*scientific concept*)?	How do the headings and subheadings relate to _____ (*scientific concept*)?	Describe how the headings and subheadings are related to _____ (*scientific concept*).
What would be another good heading for this section?	What would be a good subheading for paragraph _____?	Write a descriptive subheading for paragraph _____. How does it support the text?	Create a purposeful subheading for paragraph _____, and explain how it supports the text.
What does the _____ (*text feature*) tell/show?	Why did the author include _____ (*text feature*)?	How does _____ (*text feature*) support the text?	How does _____ (*text feature*) support your understanding of the text?
What does the _____ (*text feature*) tell/show you about _____ (*scientific concept*)?	What does the _____ (*text feature*) help you understand about _____ (*scientific concept*)?	How does the _____ (*text feature*) support your understanding of _____ (*scientific concept*)?	Use examples from the text to explain how the _____ (*text feature*) supports your understanding of _____ (*scientific concept*).

Using Text Features K–12 Alignment *(cont.)*

★	●	■	▲
What does the chart/graph/picture tell about _____ (*scientific concept/main idea*)?	How does the chart/graph/diagram/image support _____ (*scientific concept/main idea*)?	How does the chart/graph/diagram/image support _____ (*scientific concept/main idea*)?	Use examples from the text to describe how the chart/graph/diagram/image supports _____ (*scientific concept/main idea*).
How does the chart/graph/picture help you read the text?	How does the chart/graph/diagram/image help you understand the scientific ideas in the text?	How does the chart/graph/diagram/image clarify the scientific concepts in the text?	Explain how the chart/graph/diagram/image clarifies the scientific concepts in the text. Cite specific examples in your response.
What does the _____ (*text feature*) show that is not in the text?	What does the _____ (*text feature*) show that isn't included in the text?	What additional information does the _____ (*text feature*) provide that isn't included in the text? Why is it important?	Analyze any additional information the _____ (*text feature*) provides that isn't included in the text and why it is important to include.
What does the chart/graph/picture tell about?	What information does the chart/graph/diagram/image provide?	Summarize the information given in the chart/graph/diagram/image.	Use key details to summarize the information given in the chart/graph/diagram/image.
Look at the chart/graph/diagram/image. What happens first?	What are the parts/steps of the chart/graph/diagram/image?	What is the order of events for _____ (*scientific process*), according to the chart/graph/diagram/image?	Use the chart/graph/diagram/image to summarize the order of events for _____ (*scientific process*).

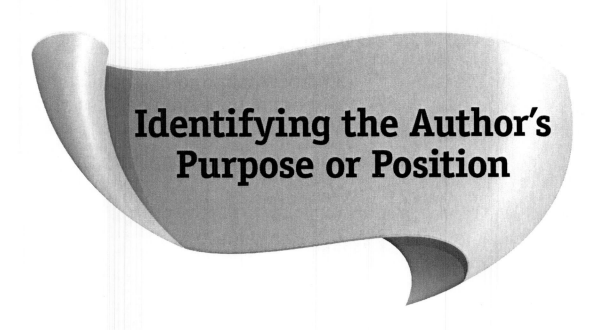

Identifying the Author's Purpose or Position

Skill Overview

Most scientific texts are written for one of two purposes: to inform or to persuade. When students learn to identify *why* an author wrote a text, they can then learn to analyze *how* the purpose or position is reflected in the author's writing. Understanding the author's purpose or position and how that point of view controls the content of a text is an important skill for readers.

An author's purpose or position affects decisions the author makes when writing, such as what facts and examples to include or exclude, what research to cite, and the language through which the information is presented. In scientific writing, readers should expect to see strong evidence to support an author's thinking, but readers must also be aware of possible author bias.

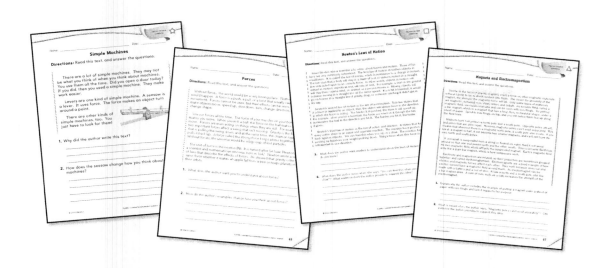

Implementing the Question Stems

This section includes 10 leveled, text-dependent question stems about identifying an author's purpose or position. You can implement these question stems by connecting them to the texts that you are reading in class.

It may seem as though using question stems would be easy, but it can be a complex task for teachers. To help you see how to implement these question stems in your classroom, this section includes student pages containing texts with sample text-dependent questions. Each of the four student pages illustrates a different complexity level.

Snapshot of Differentiating a Question

The chart below models how a single leveled question stem can be tied to science texts at four complexity levels. This snapshot also gives a quick view of how the question stems differ based on the complexity levels. However, you can also see how the question stems link to one another.

	Question Stem	Example
☆	What does the author want you to know about _____ (*scientific concept*)?	What does the author want you to know about plants?
○	What does the author want you to think/understand about _____ (*scientific concept*)?	What does the author want you to understand about animal cells?
▢	What does the author want readers to think/understand about _____ (*scientific concept*)? How do you know?	What does the author want readers to understand about animal respiration? How do you know?
△	Use evidence from the text to explain what the author wants readers to think/understand about _____ (*scientific concept*).	Use evidence from the text to explain what the author wants readers to understand about DNA.

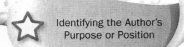

Identifying the Author's Purpose or Position Question Stems

Use these question stems to develop your own questions for students.

Why did the author write this text?

What does the author want you to know about _____ (*scientific concept*)?

What is the message of this text?

What words does the author use to make you think _____ (*opinion/conjecture*)?

Why does the author tell about _____ (*example/experiment*)? How does that support his/her purpose?

What do we still not know about _____ (*scientific concept*)?

Why does the author describe _____ (*procedure/process*)?

How does _____ (*example/fact*) change how you think about _____ (*scientific concept*)?

What other facts about _____ (*scientific concept*) are needed?

Why does the author say _____ (*quotation*)?

Name: _____ Date: _____

Simple Machines

Directions: Read this text, and answer the questions.

There are a lot of simple machines. They may not be what you think of when you think about machines. You use them all the time. Did you open a door today? If you did, then you used a simple machine. They make work easier.

Levers are one kind of simple machine. A seesaw is a lever. It uses force. The force makes an object turn around a point.

There are other kinds of simple machines, too. You just have to look for them!

1. Why did the author write this text?

_____

_____

_____

2. How does the seesaw change how you think about simple machines?

_____

_____

_____

_____

COMPLEXITY

Identifying the Author's Purpose or Position Question Stems

Use these question stems to develop your own questions for students.

Based on the title, why did the author write this text?

What does the author want you to think/understand about _____ (*scientific concept*)?

What is the author's message? How do you know?

What words does the author use to affect how you think about _____ (*scientific concept*)?

Why does the author discuss _____ (*example/experiment*)? How does that support the author's purpose?

What issues/information about _____ (*scientific concept*) are still unknown?

Why does the author describe _____ (*procedure/process*)? How does this affect his/her purpose/position?

How do the author's examples/facts change how you think about _____ (*scientific concept*) is needed?

What additional information/research about _____ (*scientific concept*) is needed?

What does the author mean when he/she says _____ (*quotation*)?

Name: _____ Date: _____

Forces

Directions: Read this text, and answer the questions.

Without forces, the world would be a very boring place. Nothing would happen. A force is a push, a pull, or a twist that usually causes movement. Forces cannot be seen, but their effects can be seen. They make objects move, speed up, slow down, turn, change direction, or change shape.

You use forces all the time. The force of your muscles on your bones makes you move. When you kick a ball, the force on the ball makes it move. Forces are even acting on things when they are still. For example, two important forces affect a swing that isn't moving. Gravity is the force that is pulling the swing down, and at the same time, the chain or rope pulls it back up. A force called the *strong force* keeps atoms together. Without forces, the universe would be a big soup of lost particles.

The unit of force is the newton (N). It is named after Sir Isaac Newton, a scientist and mathematician who was born in 1642. Newton wrote a set of laws that describe the effects of forces. He showed that gravity is the same force whether it makes an apple fall from a tree or keeps planets in their orbits.

1. What does the author want you to understand about forces?

    _____

    _____

2. How do the author's examples change how you think about forces?

    _____

    _____

    _____

COMPLEXITY

LOW ★ ● □ ▲ HIGH

Identifying the Author's Purpose or Position Question Stems

Use these question stems to develop your own questions for students.

Based on the title, explain why the author wrote this text.

What does the author want readers to think/understand about _____ (*scientific concept*)? How do you know?

What is the author's message? What evidence does he/she give to support this message?

In what ways does the author's word choice influence how you think about _____ (*scientific concept*)?

How does including _____ (*example/experiment*) support the author's purpose?

What issues/information about _____ (*scientific concept*) remain unknown?

Why does the author include information about _____ (*procedure/process*)? How does this support his/her purpose/position?

How do the author's examples/facts influence how you think about _____ (*scientific concept*)?

What additional information/research is needed to better understand _____ (*scientific concept*)?

What is meant when the author says _____ (*quotation*)? What evidence supports this idea/position?

Name: _____ Date: _____

Newton's Laws of Motion

Directions: Read this text, and answer the questions.

Isaac Newton was a scientist who wrote about forces and motion. Three of his laws are very commonly referenced. The first law of motion describes objects in equilibrium. It is called the law of inertia, which is resistance to a change in motion. The law says that a body will stay in a state of rest or uniform motion in a straight line until acted upon by an outside force. In other words, objects in motion will remain in motion; objects at rest will stay at rest. For example, a leaf on the ground will stay there unless wind, an animal, or a person moves it. Moving objects will continue moving in a straight line at the same speed. If you hit a baseball, it would go on forever in a straight line if gravity, drag, or someone catching it didn't get in its way.

Newton's second law of motion is the law of acceleration. This law states that if a force is applied to an object, then the object will always move in the direction in which the force is acting. The harder it is pushed, the more it will speed up. For example, when you hit a baseball, the force you exert on it through the bat accelerates the ball in the direction you hit it. The harder you hit it, the faster it goes.

Newton's third law of motion is the law of action and reaction. It states that for every action there is an equal and opposite reaction. The reaction force pushes back against objects. You can feel this when you sit on a chair. The reaction force pushing up balances your weight pushing down. Things move when this force is unbalanced in one direction.

1. What does the author want readers to understand about the laws of motion? How do you know?

   _____

   _____

2. What does the author mean when she says, "You can feel this when you sit on a chair"? What evidence does the author provide to support this idea?

   _____

   _____

   _____

Identifying the Author's Purpose or Position Question Stems

Use these question stems to develop your own questions for students.

Based on the title, explain why the author wrote this text. What words led you to this conclusion?

Use evidence from the text to explain what the author wants readers to think/understand about _____ (*scientific concept*).

Use the text to explain the author's message and the evidence he/she uses to support it.

Describe how the vocabulary that the author used influences your understanding of _____ (*scientific concept*).

Explain why the author includes _____ (*example/experiment*), and how it supports his/her purpose.

Identify important issues/information regarding _____ (*scientific concept*) that remain unknown.

Explain how the author's description of _____ (*procedure/ process*) supports your understanding of his/her purpose/ position.

Explain how the author's examples/facts influence your understanding of _____ (*scientific concept*).

Identify how additional information/research would help readers better understand _____ (*scientific concept*).

What is meant when the author says _____ (*quotation*)? Cite evidence the author provides to support this idea/position.

Name: _____ Date: _____

Magnets and Electromagnetism

Directions: Read this text, and answer the questions.

Similar to the force of gravity, magnets exert a force on other magnetic materials without having to be in direct contact with them. The closer the proximity of the magnet, the stronger the magnetic force will be. Only some types of materials are magnetic, including iron, steel, nickel, and cobalt. An invisible field, called a magnetic field, surrounds magnets and can be seen with iron filings. Try putting a bar magnet, which is a magnet that has a long, thin, rectangular shape, under a sheet of paper. Sprinkle iron filings on top, and you will notice them line up along the field lines.

Magnets have two poles—a north pole and a south pole. Opposite poles attract, and poles that are alike repel. However, magnetic poles can't exist separately. This means that wherever there is a magnetic north pole, a south pole also exists. If you break a magnet in half, it will become two smaller magnets, and each will have its own north and south poles.

If a magnet is suspended from a string or floated on water, then it will swing around so that one end points north and the other south. This is because Earth has its own magnetic field, which attracts the suspended magnet. Earth's magnetic field acts like a giant bar magnet, which is how compasses work.

Electricity and magnetism are related, so their properties are sometimes grouped together and called electromagnetism. Electromagnets are a good example of how electric and magnetic forces affect each other. They work because wires carrying electric current have a magnetic field around them. An electromagnet can be made with a battery and a coil of wire. It has a north and a south pole, just like a bar magnet does. A core of iron, such as a nail, increases the strength of the electromagnet.

1. Explain why the author includes the example of putting a magnet under a sheet of paper with iron filings and how it supports her purpose.

   _____

   _____

2. What is meant when the author says, "Magnetic poles can't exist separately"? Cite evidence the author provides to support this idea.

   _____

   _____

   _____

Identifying the Author's Purpose or Position K–12 Alignment

Use this chart to determine the best question stems for your different groups of students.

★	●	■	▲
Why did the author write this text?	Based on the title, why did the author write this text?	Based on the title, explain why the author wrote this text.	Based on the title, explain why the author wrote this text. What words led you to this conclusion?
What does the author want you to know about _____ (*scientific concept*)?	What does the author want you to think/understand about _____ (*scientific concept*)?	What does the author want readers to think/understand about _____ (*scientific concept*)? How do you know?	Use evidence from the text to explain what the author wants readers to think/understand about _____ (*scientific concept*).
What is the message of this text?	What is the author's message? How do you know?	What is the author's message? What evidence does he/she give to support this message?	Use the text to explain the author's message and the evidence he/she uses to support it.
What words does the author use to make you think _____ (*opinion/conjecture*)?	What words does the author use to affect how you think about _____ (*scientific concept*)?	In what ways does the author's word choice influence how you think about _____ (*scientific concept*)?	Describe how the vocabulary that the author used influences your understanding of _____ (*scientific concept*).
Why does the author tell about _____ (*example/experiment*)? How does that support his/her purpose?	Why does the author discuss _____ (*example/experiment*)? How does that support the author's purpose?	How does including _____ (*example/experiment*) support the author's purpose?	Explain why the author includes _____ (*example/experiment*) and how it supports his/her purpose.

Identifying the Author's Purpose or Position
K–12 Alignment *(cont.)*

★	●	■	▲
What do we still not know about _____ (*scientific concept*)?	What issues/information about _____ (*scientific concept*) are still unknown?	What issues/information about _____ (*scientific concept*) remain unknown?	Identify important issues/information regarding _____ (*scientific concept*) that remain unknown.
Why does the author describe _____ (*procedure/process*)?	Why does the author describe _____ (*procedure/process*)? How does this affect his/her purpose/position?	Why does the author include information about _____ (*procedure/process*)? How does this support his/her purpose/position?	Explain how the author's description of _____ (*procedure/process*) supports your understanding his/her purpose/position.
How does _____ (*example/fact*) change how you think about _____ (*scientific concept*)?	How do the author's examples/facts change how you think about _____ (*scientific concept*)?	How do the author's examples/facts influence how you think about _____ (*scientific concept*)?	Explain how the author's examples/facts influence your understanding of _____ (*scientific concept*).
What other facts about _____ (*scientific concept*) are needed?	What additional information/research about _____ (*scientific concept*) is needed?	What additional information/research is needed to better understand _____ (*scientific concept*)?	Identify how additional information/research would help readers better understand _____ (*scientific concept*).
Why does the author say _____ (*quotation*)?	What does the author mean when he/she says _____ (*quotation*)?	What is meant when the author says _____ (*quotation*)? What evidence supports this idea/position?	What is meant when the author says _____ (*quotation*)? Cite evidence the author provides to support this idea/position.

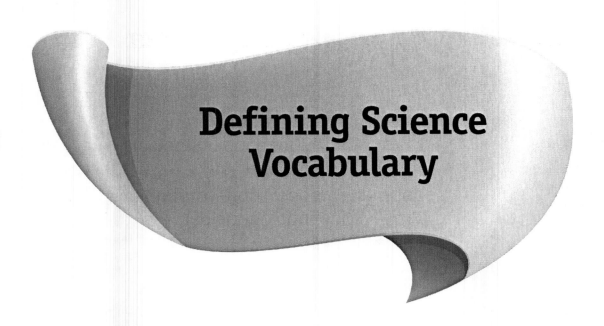

Defining Science Vocabulary

Skill Overview

Science is a subject that presents students with many new terms and ideas. This vocabulary is key to understanding the underlying scientific concepts. However, defining science vocabulary can be difficult since the terms may be unfamiliar or abstract. Sometimes, even familiar words have specific scientific definitions that vary from their everyday usage. Focusing on vocabulary helps students to both understand the scientific concepts and discuss the concepts, using appropriate terminology.

Younger students or English language learners may need extra support before reading. Teaching new vocabulary words prior to reading is an effective strategy. Teachers preview the text, find the unfamiliar words, and define and discuss these words with students. By doing this, students have some prior knowledge on which to build when these words are encountered in a text.

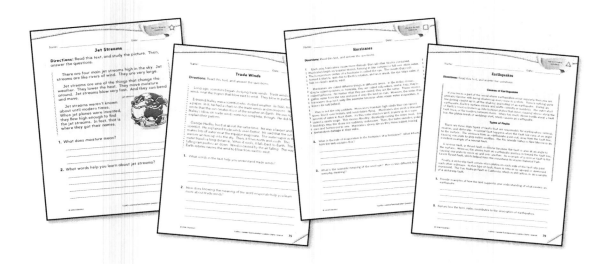

Implementing the Question Stems

This section includes 10 leveled, text-dependent question stems about scientific vocabulary. You can implement these question stems by connecting them to the texts that you are reading in class.

It may seem as though using question stems would be easy, but it can be a complex task for teachers. To help you see how to implement these question stems in your classroom, this section includes student pages containing texts with sample text-dependent questions. Each of the four student pages illustrates a different complexity level.

Snapshot of Differentiating a Question

The chart below models how a single leveled question stem can be tied to science texts at four complexity levels. This snapshot also gives a quick view of how the question stems differ based on the complexity levels. However, you can also see how the question stems link to one another.

	Question Stem	Example
☆	What does _____ (word/phrase) mean in this text?	What does *weight* mean in this text?
◯	What is the scientific meaning of _____ (word/phrase)? What is its everyday meaning?	What is the scientific meaning of *matter*? What is its everyday meaning?
▢	What is the scientific meaning of _____ (word/phrase)? How is this different from its everyday meaning?	What is the scientific meaning of *force*? How is this different from its everyday meaning?
△	Compare the scientific definition of _____ (word/phrase) with its everyday meaning.	Compare the scientific definition of *conductor* with its everyday meaning.

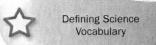

Defining Science Vocabulary Question Stems

Use these question stems to develop your own questions for students.

What does _____ (*word/phrase*) mean?

What does _____ (*word/phrase*) mean in this text?

What words or phrases do you know from the text?

What do you think _____ (*scientific symbol*) means?

How can you figure out what _____ (*word/phrase*) means?

What does _____ (*scientific term*) do in _____ (*procedure/ process*)?

What word means the same as/opposite of _____ (*word/ phrase*)?

What words help you learn about _____ (*scientific concept*)?

How does _____ (*word/phrase*) tell about _____ (*scientific concept*)?

What do you know about _____ (*scientific concept*)? How did the text help you?

Name: _____ Date: _____

Jet Streams

Directions: Read this text, and study the picture. Then, answer the questions.

There are four main jet streams high in the sky. Jet streams are like rivers of wind. They are very large.

Jet streams are one of the things that change the weather. They lower the heat. They move moisture around. Jet streams blow very fast. And they can bend and move.

jet streams

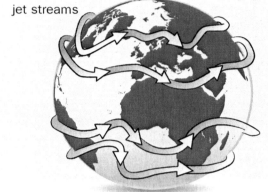

Jet streams weren't known about until modern times. When jet planes were invented, they flew high enough to find the jet streams. In fact, that is where they got their names.

1. What does *moisture* mean?

_____

_____

_____

2. What words help you learn about jet streams?

_____

_____

_____

_____

Defining Science Vocabulary Question Stems

Use these question stems to develop your own questions for students.

What is the scientific meaning of _____ (*word/phrase*)?

....

What is the scientific meaning of _____ (*word/phrase*)? What is its everyday meaning?

....

What words/phrases in the text help you understand _____ (*scientific concept*)?

....

What is the meaning of _____ (*scientific symbol*)?

....

How can you find the meaning of _____ (*word/phrase*)?

....

What is the role of _____ (*scientific term*) in _____ (*procedure/ process*)?

....

What term means the same as/opposite of _____ (*word/ phrase*)? How do you know?

....

How does knowing the meaning of _____ (*word/phrase*) help you learn more about _____ (*scientific concept*)?

....

How does _____ (*word/phrase*) describe _____ (*scientific concept*)?

....

What do you understand about _____ (*scientific concept*)? How does the text help you understand this?

Name: _____ Date: _____

Trade Winds

Directions: Read this text, and answer the questions.

Long ago, scientists began studying trade winds. Trade winds are winds near the tropics that blow east to west. They blow in patterns.

Edmond Halley was a scientist who studied weather. In 1686, he wrote a paper. In it, he had a chart on the trade winds and monsoons. Halley wrote that the sun creates most of the weather on Earth. He was right. Halley's ideas on trade winds were not complete, though. He did not explain their pattern.

George Hadley lived at about the same time. He was a lawyer and a scientist. He explained trade winds even better. He said that the sun makes lots of water near the equator evaporate. The water vapor in the warmer air rises up into the sky. Then, it flows north and south. This water travels a long distance. When it cools, it falls back to Earth. The falling rain pushes air down. Wind is caused by the air falling. The way Earth rotates causes the wind to blow from east to west.

1. What words in the text help you understand trade winds?

   _____

   _____

   _____

2. How does knowing the meaning of the word *evaporate* help you learn more about trade winds?

   _____

   _____

   _____

COMPLEXITY

LOW ★ ● □ ▲ HIGH

Defining Science Vocabulary Question Stems

Use these question stems to develop your own questions for students.

What is the meaning of _____ (*word/phrase*) in terms of _____ (*scientific concept*)?

What is the scientific meaning of _____ (*word/phrase*)? How is this different from its everyday meaning?

How does the scientific vocabulary in the text help you better understand _____ (*scientific concept*)?

What is the scientific meaning of _____ (*scientific symbol*)? How do you know?

What word parts in _____ (*word/phrase*) helped you figure out its meaning?

What is the role of _____ (*scientific term*) in _____ (*procedure/process*)? What information from the text explains this?

Based on the text, what scientific term means the same as/opposite of _____ (*word/phrase*)?

How does knowing the meaning of _____ (*word/phrase*) help you understand _____ (*scientific concept*)?

How does _____ (*word/phrase*) accurately describe _____ (*scientific concept*)?

Explain your understanding of _____ (*scientific concept*). How does the text support this understanding?

Name: _____ Date: _____

Hurricanes

Directions: Read this text, and answer the questions.

Each year, hurricanes cause more damage than all other storms combined. Hurricanes begin as tropical storms, forming in late summer or fall over warm water. The low-pressure center of a hurricane is called the eye. The clouds that rush toward it start to spin due to Earth's rotation, and as a result, the eye stays calm: it has no clouds and no wind.

Hurricanes are called different things in different areas. In the Indian Ocean, they're called cyclones, in Australia, they are called willy-willies, and in Asia, they're called typhoons. No matter what they are called, they act the same. These storms gather water from the sea and pour it onto the land as rain. However, the water that hurricanes drop isn't salty like seawater because when ocean water evaporates, it leaves its salt behind.

Rain is not the only problem. Hurricanes maintain high winds that can uproot trees, knock over homes, and send debris flying. Hurricanes also push a massive amount of water in front them. As this water reaches land, it piles up in a wave called a storm surge. This causes flooding, drastically raising the water level. Small buildings near the shore are suddenly underwater. Then, the water recedes, pulling cars and homes out to sea. Hurricanes slowly die as they move inland, leaving tremendous damage in their wake.

1. What is the role of evaporation in the formation of a hurricane? What information from the text explains this?

   _____

   _____

   _____

2. What is the scientific meaning of the word *eye*? How is this different from its everyday meaning?

   _____

   _____

   _____

   _____

Defining Science Vocabulary Question Stems

Use these question stems to develop your own questions for students.

What is the meaning of _____ (*word/phrase*) in terms of _____ (*scientific concept*)? Use evidence from the text to support your answer.

Compare the scientific definition of _____ (*word/phrase*) with its everyday meaning.

Use examples from the text to describe how the scientific vocabulary contributes to your understanding of _____ (*scientific concept*).

Explain how the text helps you understand what _____ (*scientific symbol*) means.

Explain how the word parts in _____ (*word/phrase*) helped you determine its meaning in this context.

Describe how the text explains the role of _____ (*scientific term*) in _____ (*procedure/process*).

Explain how the text clarifies that_____ (*scientific term*) means the same as/opposite of _____ (*scientific term*).

Explain how the meaning of _____ (*word/phrase*) supports your understanding of _____ (*scientific concept*).

Explain how _____ (*word/phrase*) contributes to the description of _____ (*scientific concept*).

Provide examples of how the text supports your understanding of _____ (*scientific concept*).

Name: _____ Date: _____

Earthquakes

Directions: Read this text, and answer the questions.

Causes of Earthquakes

If you live in a part of the world where earthquakes occur regularly, then you are probably familiar with being shaken up every once in a while. There's nothing quite like getting caught up in all the shaking and rolling of an earthquake. During an earthquake, Earth's surface moves and shifts violently or suddenly. The outer shell of Earth's crust is broken up into tectonic plates that move, causing stress along the fault lines, or the borders between them. When too much stress builds along a fault line, the plates break or suddenly shift, which causes an earthquake.

Types of Faults

There are three main types of faults that are responsible for earthquakes: normal, reverse, and strike-slip. A normal fault happens when the fault line runs at an angle to the surface. The stresses from an earthquake push out, away from the fault line, causing one plate to drop below another. The Rio Grande Valley in New Mexico is an excellent example of a normal fault.

A reverse fault, or thrust fault, is similar because the fault is also at an angle to the surface. However, the stress from an earthquake pushes in toward the fault line, causing one plate to move up and over another. An example of a reverse fault is the Lewis Thrust Fault, which helped form the mountains in Glacier National Park.

Finally, a strike-slip fault occurs when plates on each side of the fault slip past each other sideways. In this type of fault, there is little or no upward or downward movement. The San Andreas Fault in California, which is still active, is an example of a strike-slip fault.

1. Provide examples of how the text supports your understanding of what causes an earthquake.

   _____

   _____

   _____

2. Explain how the term *plates* contributes to the description of earthquakes.

   _____

   _____

Defining Science Vocabulary K–12 Alignment

Use this chart to determine the best question stems for your different groups of students.

★	●	■	▲
What does _____ (*word/phrase*) mean?	What is the scientific meaning of _____ (*word/phrase*)?	What is the meaning of _____ (*word/phrase*) in terms of _____ (*scientific concept*)?	What is the meaning of _____ (*word/phrase*) in terms of _____ (*scientific concept*)? Use evidence from the text to support your answer.
What does _____ (*word/phrase*) mean in this text?	What is the scientific meaning of _____ (*word/phrase*)? What is its everyday meaning?	What is the scientific meaning of _____ (*word/phrase*)? How is this different from its everyday meaning?	Compare the scientific definition of _____ (*word/phrase*) with its everyday meaning.
What words or phrases do you know from the text?	What words/phrases in the text help you understand _____ (*scientific concept*)?	How does the scientific vocabulary in the text help you better understand _____ (*scientific concept*)?	Use examples from the text to describe how the scientific vocabulary contributes to your understanding of _____ (*scientific concept*).
What do you think _____ (*scientific symbol*) means?	What is the meaning of _____ (*scientific symbol*)?	What is the scientific meaning of _____ (*scientific symbol*)? How do you know?	Explain how the text helps you understand what _____ (*scientific symbol*) means.
How can you figure out what _____ (*word/phrase*) means?	How can you find the meaning of _____ (*word/phrase*)?	What word parts in _____ (*word/phrase*) helped you figure out its meaning?	Explain how the word parts in _____ (*word/phrase*) helped you determine its meaning in this context.

Defining Science Vocabulary K–12 Alignment (cont.)

⭐	⬤	◼	▲
What does _____ (*scientific term*) do in _____ (*procedure/ process*)?	What is the role of _____ (*scientific term*) in _____ (*procedure/ process*)?	What is the role of _____ (*scientific term*) in _____ (*procedure/ process*)? What information from the text explains this?	Describe how the text explains the role of _____ (*scientific term*) in _____ (*procedure/ process*).
What word means the same as/ opposite of _____ (*word/phrase*)?	What term means the same as/ opposite of _____ (*word/phrase*)? How do you know?	Based on the text, what scientific term means the same as/ opposite of _____ (*word/phrase*)?	Explain how the text clarifies that _____ (*scientific term*) means the same as/opposite of _____ (*scientific term*).
What words help you learn about _____ (*scientific concept*)?	How does knowing the meaning of _____ (*word/ phrase*) help you learn more about _____ (*scientific concept*)?	How does knowing the meaning of _____ (*word/phrase*) help you understand _____ (*scientific concept*)?	Explain how the meaning of _____ (*word/ phrase*) supports your understanding of _____ (*scientific concept*).
How does _____ (*word/phrase*) tell about _____ (*scientific concept*)?	How does _____ (*word/phrase*) describe _____ (*scientific concept*)?	How does _____ (*word/phrase*) accurately describe _____ (*scientific concept*)?	Explain how _____ (*word/ phrase*) contributes to the description of _____ (*scientific concept*).
What do you know about _____ (*scientific concept*)? How did the text help you?	What do you understand about _____ (*scientific concept*)? How does the text help you understand this?	Explain your understanding of _____ (*scientific concept*). How does the text support this understanding?	Provide examples of how the text supports your understanding of _____ (*scientific concept*).

Drawing Conclusions

Skill Overview

Scientists draw conclusions by examining and evaluating data as well as experimental results. After experiments, scientists often directly state the relationships between the variables they were investigating. Students should learn to analyze conclusions to verify that scientists' statements are valid based on the given data.

When a hypothesis has been given, the conclusions should refer back to it by stating whether the data support the hypothesis. It is important for students to realize that an experiment is not wrong when a hypothesis is not supported by the data.

Students can also analyze experimental procedures when considering scientific conclusions. Students can refer to written procedures to determine what factors may have affected the experimental results or to make suggestions for improving experimental methods.

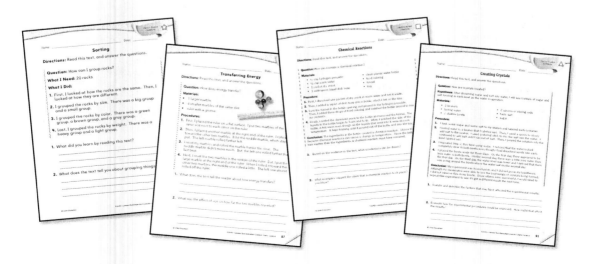

Implementing the Question Stems

This section includes 10 leveled, text-dependent question stems about drawing conclusions. You can implement these question stems by connecting them to the texts that you are reading in class.

It may seem as though using question stems would be easy, but it can be a complex task for teachers. To help you see how to implement these question stems in your classroom, this section includes student pages containing texts with sample text-dependent questions. Each of the four student pages illustrates a different complexity level.

Snapshot of Differentiating a Question

The chart below models how a single leveled question stem can be tied to science texts at four complexity levels. This snapshot also gives a quick view of how the question stems differ based on the complexity levels. However, you can also see how the question stems link to one another.

	Question Stem	Example
☆	What does the text say about _____ (*hypothesis*)?	What does the text say about why the water is cold?
○	What supports the hypothesis that _____ (*hypothesis*)?	What supports the hypothesis that the water evaporated?
▢	How do the observations/data support the hypothesis that _____ (*hypothesis*)?	How do the observations support the hypothesis that the metal is not magnetic?
△	Use examples from the text to describe how the observations/data support the hypothesis that _____ (*hypothesis*).	Use examples from the text to describe how the observations support the hypothesis that the substance is a nonmetal.

Drawing Conclusions Question Stems

Use these question stems to develop your own questions for students.

What happened? Is that what the author thought would happen?

What does the text tell about what happened?

What does the text say about _____ (*hypothesis*)?

What does the test show?

What happened when _____ (*variable*) changed/was added/was removed?

What happens when _____ (*factor affecting the results*) was changed?

What does the text tell you about _____ (*scientific concept*)?

What did you learn by reading this text?

What words/numbers tell more about _____ (*hypothesis/claim*)?

How could you change the test to make it better?

Name: _____   Date: _____

Sorting

Directions: Read this text, and answer the questions.

Question: How can I group rocks?

What I Need: 20 rocks

What I Did:

1. First, I looked at how the rocks are the same. Then, I looked at how they are different.

2. I grouped the rocks by size. There was a big group and a small group.

3. I grouped the rocks by color. There was a green group, a brown group, and a gray group.

4. Last, I grouped the rocks by weight. There was a heavy group and a light group.

1. What did you learn by reading this text?

   _____

   _____

   _____

2. What does the text tell you about grouping things?

   _____

   _____

   _____

Drawing Conclusions Question Stems

Use these question stems to develop your own questions for students.

Do the results support the hypothesis? If so, how?

What evidence supports the hypothesis?

What supports the hypothesis that _____ (*hypothesis*)?

What does the experiment show?

What is the effect of _____ (*independent variable*) on _____ (*dependent variable*)?

What may have affected the results?

What does the text tell the reader about _____ (*scientific concept*)?

What conclusions can you draw from this text?

What data/examples can you find to support _____ (*hypothesis/claim*)?

How could the experiment be improved?

Name: _____ Date: _____

Transferring Energy

Directions: Read this text, and answer the questions.

Question: How does energy transfer?

Materials:

- 1 larger marble
- 4 smaller marbles of the same size
- ruler with a groove

Procedures:

1. First, I placed the ruler on a flat surface. I put two marbles of the same size next to each other on the ruler.

2. Then, I placed another marble at the right end of the ruler. I rolled it toward the other two marbles. It hit the middle marble, which stayed put. The left marble rolled farther left.

3. I reset my marbles and rolled the marble harder this time. The middle marble didn't move much. But, the left one rolled farther than last time.

4. Next, I reset the two marbles in the middle of the ruler. But, I put the large marble at the right end of the ruler. When I rolled it toward the other two marbles, the middle one rolled a little. The left one almost rolled off the ruler.

1. What does the text tell the reader about how energy transfers?

_____

_____

2. What was the effect of size on how far the two marbles traveled?

_____

_____

_____

LOW ★ ● □ ▲ HIGH

Drawing Conclusions Question Stems

Use these question stems to develop your own questions for students.

Do the experimental results support the hypothesis? How do you know?

- -

How does the evidence in this text support the hypothesis?

- -

How do the observations/data support the hypothesis that _____ (*hypothesis*)?

- -

What does the experiment show? What is the relationship between the variables?

- -

How does _____ (*independent variable*) affect _____ (*dependent variable*)? How do you know?

- -

What factors/conditions may have affected the results of the experiment?

- -

What do the data in this text tell the reader about _____ (*scientific concept*)?

- -

Based on the evidence in the text, what conclusions can be drawn?

- -

What data/examples support _____ (*hypothesis/claim*)? How do you know?

- -

Explain how the experimental procedures could be improved.

Name: _____ Date: _____

Chemical Reactions

Directions: Read this text, and answer the questions.

Question: How can I create a chemical reaction?

Materials:

- ½ cup hydrogen peroxide
- ½ cup warm water
- 1 packet dry yeast
- 1 tablespoon liquid dish soap
- clean plastic water bottle
- food coloring
- funnel
- tray

Procedure:

1. First, I dissolved one packet of dry yeast in warm water and set it aside.

2. Then, I added a squirt of dish soap into a bottle, which I set on the tray.

3. I put the funnel in the bottle opening and poured in the hydrogen peroxide. Then, I added three drops of food coloring and swished the bottle around to mix its contents.

4. Finally, I added the dissolved yeast to the bottle and removed the funnel. The liquids in the bottle began to foam and froth. When I touched the side of the bottle, it felt warm even though all the liquids that went into it were at room temperature. It kept foaming until it poured out of the bottle and into the tray.

Conclusion: The ingredients in the bottle created a chemical reaction. I know this because chemical reactions can cause a change in temperature. Since the bottle was warmer than the ingredients, a chemical reaction must have occurred.

1. Based on the evidence in the text, what conclusions can be drawn?

   _____

   _____

   _____

2. What examples support the claim that a chemical reaction took place? How do you know?

   _____

   _____

   _____

Drawing Conclusions Question Stems

Use these question stems to develop your own questions for students.

Use evidence from the text to analyze whether the experimental results support the hypothesis.

Cite specific examples from the text to describe how the evidence supports the hypothesis.

Use examples from the text to describe how the observations/ data support the hypothesis that _____ (*hypothesis*).

Describe the outcome of the experiment, and analyze the relationship between the variables.

Explain how you know what effect _____ (*independent variable*) has on _____ (*dependent variable*).

Analyze and describe the factors/conditions that may have affected the experimental results.

Identify the data in this text that explain _____ (*scientific concept*) to the reader.

Summarize the conclusions that can be drawn from this text. Support your answer with evidence from the text.

Identify data/examples that best supports the author's hypothesis/claim.

Evaluate how the experimental procedures could be improved. How might that affect the results?

Name: _____ Date: _____

Creating Crystals

Directions: Read this text, and answer the questions.

Question: How are crystals created?

Hypothesis: After dissolving sugar and salt into water, I will see crystals of sugar and salt forming in each bowl as the water evaporates.

Materials:

- 2 beakers
- boiling water
- 2 shallow bowls
- 2 spoons or stirring rods
- table salt
- sugar

Procedure:

1. I took some sugar and some salt to my station and labeled each container.

2. I boiled water in a beaker that I labeled *salt*. Then, I used a spoon to slowly add salt to the beaker. I used a stirring stick to mix the salt into the water. I continued to add salt until I ran out of salt. Then, I poured the solution into the bowl labeled *salt*.

3. I repeated Step 2, this time using sugar. I noticed that the water looked completely clear in both bowls even though I had dissolved solids into each.

4. I placed the bowls aside for three days. On the first day, there appeared to be less water in both bowls. On the second day, there was a little less water than the first day. On the third day, the water level was lower and I noticed that there was a ring around the bowls where the water sat on the second day.

Conclusion: My experiment was inconclusive, and I did not prove my hypothesis. Although my classmates were able to see the beginnings of crystals being formed, I did not observe this in my bowls. Since others were successful, I would need to repeat this experiment to see if I get a different result the next time.

1. Analyze and describe the factors that may have affected the experimental results.

_____

_____

2. Evaluate how the experimental procedures could be improved. How might that affect the results?

_____

_____

Drawing Conclusions K–12 Alignment

Use this chart to determine the best question stems for your different groups of students.

★	●	■	▲
What happened? Is that what the author thought would happen?	Do the results support the hypothesis? If so, how?	Do the experimental results support the hypothesis? How do you know?	Use evidence from the text to analyze whether the experimental results support the hypothesis.
What does the text tell about what happened?	What evidence supports the hypothesis?	How does the evidence in this text support the hypothesis?	Cite specific examples from the text to describe how the evidence supports the hypothesis.
What does the text say about _____ (hypothesis)?	What supports the hypothesis that _____ (hypothesis)?	How do the observations/ data support the hypothesis that _____ (hypothesis)?	Use examples from the text to describe how the observations/data support the hypothesis that _____ (hypothesis).
What does the test show?	What does the experiment show?	What does the experiment show? What is the relationship between the variables?	Describe the outcome of the experiment, and analyze the relationship between the variables.
What happened when _____ (variable) changed/ was added/was removed?	What is the effect of _____ (independent variable) on _____ (dependent variable)?	How does _____ (independent variable) affect _____ (dependent variable)? How do you know?	Explain how you know what effect _____ (independent variable) has on _____ (dependent variable).

Drawing Conclusions K–12 Alignment (cont.)

★	●	■	▲
What happens when _____ (*factor affecting the results*) was changed?	What may have affected the results?	What factors/conditions may have affected the results of the experiment?	Analyze and describe the factors/conditions that may have affected the experimental results.
What does the text tell you about _____ (*scientific concept*)?	What does the text tell the reader about _____ (*scientific concept*)?	What do the data in this text tell the reader about _____ (*scientific concept*)?	Identify the data in this text that explain _____ (*scientific concept*) to the reader.
What did you learn by reading this text?	What conclusions can you draw from this text?	Based on the evidence in the text, what conclusions can be drawn?	Summarize the conclusions that can be drawn from this text. Support your answer with evidence from the text.
What words/numbers tell more about _____ (*hypothesis/claim*)?	What data/examples can you find to support _____ (*hypothesis/claim*)?	What data/examples support _____ (*hypothesis/claim*)? How do you know?	Identify data/examples that best support the author's hypothesis/claim.
How could you change the test to make it better?	How could the experiment be improved?	Explain how the experimental procedures could be improved.	Evaluate how the experimental procedures could be improved. How might that affect the results?

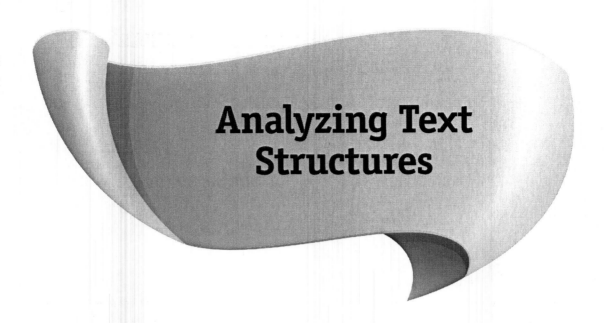

Analyzing Text Structures

Skill Overview

Text structures are how authors organize information in texts. When students learn to identify the organizational patterns in texts, they can structure their own thinking using the same patterns, which will help them better understand the information.

There are five text structures typically used in scientific texts: sequence, description, cause/effect, compare/contrast, and problem/solution. Sequence texts are organized chronologically or in a series of steps. Descriptive texts provide details to explain or describe ideas and concepts. Cause/effect texts present events and identify the causes or effects of those events. The compare/contrast structure identifies similarities and differences between ideas. Finally, the problem/solution structure introduces problems and describes possible solutions. Each of these text structures has key features and signal words that students can use to identify them.

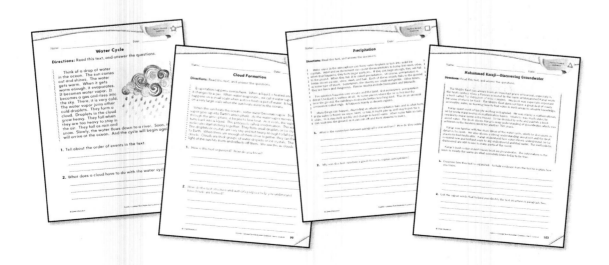

Implementing the Question Stems

This section includes 10 leveled, text-dependent question stems about analyzing text structures. You can implement these question stems by connecting them to the texts that you are reading in class.

It may seem as though using question stems would be easy, but it can be a complex task for teachers. To help you see how to implement these question stems in your classroom, this section includes student pages containing texts with sample text-dependent questions. Each of the four student pages illustrates a different complexity level.

Snapshot of Differentiating a Question

The chart below models how a single leveled question stem can be tied to science texts at four complexity levels. This snapshot also gives a quick view of how the question stems differ based on the complexity levels. However, you can also see how the question stems link to one another.

	Question Stem	Example
☆	How does the order of the text help you learn about _____ (*scientific concept*)?	How does the order of the text help you learn about rain?
○	How does the order in which the text is arranged help you understand _____ (*scientific concept*)?	How does the order in which the text is arranged help you understand the water cycle?
▢	How does the sequence in which the text is arranged help clarify _____ (*scientific concept*)?	How does the sequence in which the text is arranged help clarify factors that affect weather?
△	Explain how the sequence in which the text is arranged clarifies your understanding of _____ (*scientific concept*).	Explain how the sequence in which the text is arranged clarifies your understanding of atmospheric pressure.

Analyzing Text Structures Question Stems

Use these question stems to develop your own questions for students.

How is the text organized?

Tell about the order of events in the text.

What words help you know the text is _____ (*text structure*)?

How do the headings help group things in the text?

How does the order of the text help you learn about _____ (*scientific concept*)?

How are sentences _____ and _____ connected?

Was _____ (*text structure*) a good way to help you learn about _____ (*scientific concept*)? Why or why not?

What hints are there about how the text is laid out?

What does _____ (*scientific concept*) have to do with _____ (*scientific concept*)?

How did the author help you learn about _____ (*scientific concept*)?

Name: _____   Date: _____

Water Cycle

Directions: Read this text, and answer the questions.

Think of a drop of water in the ocean. The sun comes out and shines. The water gets warm. When it gets warm enough, it evaporates. It becomes water vapor. It becomes a gas and rises into the sky. There, it is very cold. The water vapor joins other cold droplets. They form a cloud. Droplets in the cloud grow heavy. They fall when they are too heavy to stay in the air. They fall as rain and snow. Slowly, the water flows down to a river. Soon, it will arrive at the ocean. And the cycle will begin again.

1. Tell about the order of events in the text.

_____

_____

_____

2. What does a cloud have to do with the water cycle?

_____

_____

_____

Analyzing Text Structures Question Stems

Use these question stems to develop your own questions for students.

How is this text organized? How do you know?

Tell how paragraph _____ is organized.

What signal words help you know the text is _____ (*text structure*)?

How do the headings help you understand the text structure?

How does the order in which the text is arranged help you understand _____ (*scientific concept*)?

What is the connection between paragraphs _____ and _____?

Was this text structure a good choice to explain _____ (*scientific concept*)? Why or why not?

What hints are given about the text's structure in the opening sentence?

How are _____ (*scientific concept*) and _____ (*scientific concept*) connected?

How do the text structure and author's purpose help you understand _____ (*scientific concept*)?

Name: _____ Date: _____

Cloud Formation

Directions: Read this text, and answer the questions.

Evaporation happens everywhere. When a liquid is heated enough, it changes to a gas. When water evaporates, we call it water vapor. It happens on a small scale when a stove heats a pot of water. It happens on a very large scale when the sun heats water in the oceans.

When the sun heats the oceans, some water becomes vapor. The vapor goes up into Earth's atmosphere. As the water vapor moves up through the atmosphere, it begins to lose heat. As it cools, the vapor turns back into a liquid. This process is called condensation. The water molecules start sticking together. They form small droplets or ice crystals. The droplets or crystals are very tiny and not heavy enough to fall back to Earth. When there are enough of them close together, they can form clouds. Clouds are thick groups of water droplets or ice crystals. The light of the sun hits them and reflects off them. We see this as clouds.

1. How is this text organized? How do you know?

   _____

   _____

   _____

   _____

2. How do the text structure and author's purpose help you understand how clouds are formed?

   _____

   _____

   _____

   _____

Analyzing Text Structures Question Stems

Use these question stems to develop your own questions for students.

How is this text organized? Use examples from the text to show how you know.

Describe how paragraph _____ is organized.

What signal words help you recognize the text structure in paragraph _____?

How do the headings support the text's structure?

How does the sequence in which the text is arranged help clarify _____ (*scientific concept*)?

What is the connection between paragraphs _____ and _____? How do they relate?

Why was this text structure a good/poor choice to explain _____ (*scientific concept*)?

How does the opening sentence provide clues about the text's structure?

Describe the relationship between _____ (*scientific concept*) and _____ (*scientific concept*).

How do the text structure and the author's purpose work together to help you understand _____ (*scientific concept*)?

Name: _____ Date: _____

Precipitation

Directions: Read this text, and answer the questions.

Water vapor in the atmosphere can form water droplets or turn into solid ice crystals. Wind and air movement can cause these particles to bump into each other. When that happens, they form larger particles. If they get large enough, they will fall to the ground. When they fall, it is called precipitation. Of course, precipitation is better known as rain, snow, sleet, and hail. Each of these usually falls to the ground in some type of storm. Sometimes, the storms are small and gentle. Other times, they are fierce and dangerous. Fiercer storms include hurricanes and blizzards.

Precipitation happens over oceans and the land. But sometimes, precipitation doesn't hit Earth's surface at all. In some places where the air is hot and dry near the ground, the raindrops evaporate before touching land. This is an unusual occurrence called *virga*. It happens mainly in desert regions.

Many things can happen, depending on where precipitation falls and in what form. If the water is frozen as snow, sleet, or hail, it might pile up and stay frozen for a while. Or it may melt quickly and change to liquid water. When water falls as rain, it can soak into the ground, or it can run off and form streams or rivers.

1. What is the connection between paragraphs one and two? How do they relate?

   _____

   _____

   _____

   _____

2. Why was this text structure a good choice to explain precipitation?

   _____

   _____

   _____

   _____

   _____

COMPLEXITY

LOW   HIGH

Analyzing Text Structures Question Stems

Use these question stems to develop your own questions for students.

Describe how this text is organized. Include evidence from the text to explain how you know.

Describe how paragraph _____ is organized, and explain how you determined this.

List the signal words that helped you identify the text structure in paragraph _____.

Evaluate and explain how the headings communicate the text's structure.

Explain how the sequence in which the text is arranged clarifies your understanding of _____ (*scientific concept*).

Analyze and describe the relationship between paragraphs _____ and _____.

In what ways does the text structure support the explanation of _____ (*scientific concept*)?

Explain how the opening sentence/paragraph provides clues about the text's structure.

Analyze and describe the relationship between _____ (*scientific concept*) and _____ (*scientific concept*) in the text.

In what ways do the text structure and the author's purpose work together? How do the two contribute to your understanding of _____ (*scientific concept*)?

Name: _____ Date: _____

Mohammed Karaji—Discovering Groundwater

Directions: Read this text, and answer the questions.

The Middle East has always been an important place of learning, especially in the tenth century when a Persian scientist by the name of Mohammed Karaji wrote a book called *The Extraction of Hidden Waters*. His book was especially important because of where he lived. The Middle East does not have a great deal of easily accessible water, so knowing how to find water in such areas is valuable knowledge.

Karaji spent most of his life working in Baghdad. He was mainly a mathematician, so he wrote many books on mathematics topics. When he was much older, he needed to make some extra money. So he decided to write and publish a book about water. The book shows Karaji's deep understanding of groundwater, which was unknown in the Western world for another 700 years.

Karaji was familiar with the main ideas of the water cycle, which he discusses in detail in his book. He also shows a strong understanding about soil and the best places to find freshwater. Karaji understood how water moves underground, so he invented new and brilliant ways to dig underground and find water. The methods he discovered are still in use in many parts of the world.

Karaji's book is the oldest known book on groundwater. The information in the book is mostly the same as what scientists know today to be true.

1. Describe how this text is organized. Include evidence from the text to explain how you know.

_____
_____
_____
_____

2. List the signal words that helped you identify the text structure in paragraph two.

_____
_____
_____
_____

Analyzing Text Structures K–12 Alignment

Use this chart to determine the best question stems for your different groups of students.

★	●	■	▲
How is the text organized?	How is this text organized? How do you know?	How is this text organized? Use examples from the text to show how you know.	Describe how this text is organized. Include evidence from the text to explain how you know.
Tell about the order of events in the text.	Tell how paragraph _____ is organized.	Describe how paragraph _____ is organized.	Describe how paragraph _____ is organized, and explain how you determined this.
What words help you know the text is _____ (text structure)?	What signal words help you know the text is _____ (text structure)?	What signal words help you recognize the text structure in paragraph _____?	List the signal words that helped you identify the text structure in paragraph _____.
How do the headings help group things in the text?	How do the headings help you understand the text structure?	How do the headings support the text's structure?	Evaluate and explain how the headings communicate the text's structure.
How does the order of the text help you learn about _____ (scientific concept)?	How does the order in which the text is arranged help you understand _____ (scientific concept)?	How does the sequence in which the text is arranged help clarify _____ (scientific concept)?	Explain how the sequence in which the text is arranged clarifies your understanding of _____ (scientific concept).

Analyzing Text Structures K–12 Alignment *(cont.)*

★	●	■	▲
How are sentences _____ and _____ connected?	What is the connection between paragraphs _____ and _____?	What is the connection between paragraphs _____ and _____? How do they relate?	Analyze and describe the relationship between paragraphs _____ and _____.
Was _____ (*text structure*) a good way to help you learn about _____ (*scientific concept*)? Why or why not?	Was this text structure a good choice to explain _____ (*scientific concept*)? Why or why not?	Why was this text structure a good/ poor choice to explain _____ (*scientific concept*)?	In what ways does the text structure support the explanation of _____ (*scientific concept*)?
What hints are there about how the text is laid out?	What hints are given about the text's structure in the opening sentence?	How does the opening sentence provide clues about the text's structure?	Explain how the opening sentence/paragraph provides clues about the text's structure.
What does _____ (*scientific concept*) have to do with _____ (*scientific concept*)?	How are _____ (*scientific concept*) and _____ (*scientific concept*) connected?	Describe the relationship between _____ (*scientific concept*) and _____ (*scientific concept*).	Analyze and describe the relationship between _____ (*scientific concept*) and _____ (*scientific concept*) in the text.
How did the author help you learn about _____ (*scientific concept*)?	How do the text structure and author's purpose help you understand _____ (*scientific concept*)?	How do the text structure and the author's purpose work together to help you understand _____ (*scientific concept*)?	In what ways do the text structure and the author's purpose work together? How do the two contribute to your understanding of _____ (*scientific concept*)?

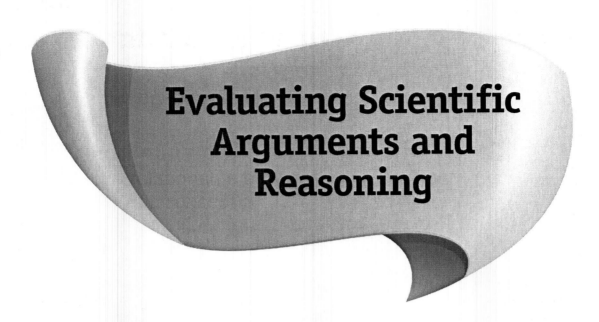

Evaluating Scientific Arguments and Reasoning

Skill Overview

Scientific arguments are created to answer scientific questions. These arguments can be tested. They should include the authors' or scientists' claims, factual evidence, and logical reasoning. Students can evaluate arguments and reasoning when they determine whether the authors' or scientists' evidence supports their claims. Students might consider the assumptions or evidence behind hypotheses, the experimental methods and procedures, and the conclusions of experiments in their evaluations. Students might also consider whether other scientists agree with the arguments. Learning to evaluate arguments and reasoning is an important component in identifying the best scientific explanations or solutions. This type of analysis teaches students to be critical thinkers.

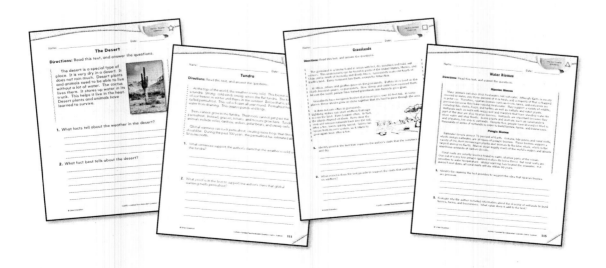

Implementing the Question Stems

This section includes 10 leveled, text-dependent question stems about evaluating scientific arguments and reasoning. You can implement these question stems by connecting them to the texts that you are reading in class.

It may seem as though using question stems would be easy, but it can be a complex task for teachers. To help you see how to implement these question stems in your classroom, this section includes student pages containing texts with sample text-dependent questions. Each of the four student pages illustrates a different complexity level.

Snapshot of Differentiating a Question

The chart below models how a single leveled question stem can be tied to science texts at four complexity levels. This snapshot also gives a quick view of how the question stems differ based on the complexity levels. However, you can also see how the question stems link to one another.

	Question Stem	Example
☆	What does _____ (information/ fact) tell about _____ (scientific concept)?	What does the size of the planets tell about the solar system?
○	How does the information about _____ (scientific concept) support the argument/claim?	How does the information about flowers' parts support the claim that each part is essential?
□	How does the information about _____ (scientific concept) help support the author's/scientist's argument/claim?	How does the information about the nervous system help support the author's claim that the nervous system affects other systems?
△	Cite specific examples of how the information about _____ (scientific concept) helps support the author's/scientist's argument/claim.	Cite specific examples of how the information about chemical reactions helps support the author's argument that combustion is a chemical reaction.

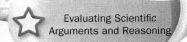 
Evaluating Scientific Arguments and Reasoning Question Stems

Use these question stems to develop your own questions for students.

What facts tell about _____ (*scientific concept*)?

What fact best tells about _____ (*scientific concept*)?

What reasons does the text give for _____ (*argument/claim*)?

What words/sentences explain _____ (*argument/claim*)?

What other words/sentences tell about _____ (*argument/claim*)?

What does _____ (*information/fact*) tell about _____ (*scientific concept*)?

Why does the author say _____ (*information/fact*)?

What would you add to the text to make it better?

Do others agree with the text? If so, who?

If you know _____ (*fact*), what do you know about _____ (*argument/claim*)?

Name: _____ Date: _____

The Desert

Directions: Read this text, and answer the questions.

The desert is a special type of place. It is very dry in a desert. It does not rain much. Desert plants and animals need to be able to live without a lot of water. The cactus lives there. It stores up water in its trunk. This helps it live in the heat. Desert plants and animals have learned to survive.

1. What facts tell about the weather in the desert?

_____

_____

_____

_____

2. What fact best tells about the desert?

_____

_____

_____

_____

COMPLEXITY

Evaluating Scientific Arguments and Reasoning Question Stems

Use these question stems to develop your own questions for students.

What facts does the author use to support _____ (*scientific concept*)?

Which facts best support the author's/scientist's reasoning?

What reasons are given for _____ (*argument/claim*)?

What words/sentences support the author's/scientist's argument/claim?

What proof is in the text to support the author's/scientist's argument/claim?

How does the information about _____ (*scientific concept*) support the argument/claim?

Why does the author include information about _____ (*scientific concept*)?

What else could have been added to improve the text?

What other scientists agree with _____ (*author/scientist*)?

If you know _____ (*fact*), what can you say about _____ (*argument/claim*)?

Name: _____ Date: _____

Tundra

Directions: Read this text, and answer the questions.

At the top of the world, the weather is very cold. This biome is called a tundra. Strong, cold winds sweep across the flat tundra. The top layer of soil freezes in winter and thaws in the summer. Below that is a layer called permafrost. This soil is frozen all year round. Permafrost keeps water from draining. This creates ponds and bogs.

Trees cannot grow in the tundra. Their roots cannot get past the permafrost. Instead, grasses, lichens, and mosses grow here. Tundra animals include voles, caribou, wolves, polar bears, and snowy owls.

Global warming can melt permafrost, creating more bogs than there should be. During the past 100 years, the permafrost has retreated about 50 miles north.

1. What sentences support the author's claim that the weather is cold on the tundra?

_____

_____

_____

2. What proof is in the text to support the author's claim that global warming melts permafrost?

_____

_____

_____

_____

COMPLEXITY

LOW ★ ● □ ▲ HIGH

Evaluating Scientific Arguments and Reasoning Question Stems

Use these question stems to develop your own questions for students.

How does the author use facts to support _____ (*scientific concept*)?

What evidence from the text strongly supports the author's/ scientist's reasoning?

What reasons does the text provide to support _____ (*argument/claim*)?

How does the information in sentence/paragraph _____ support the author's/scientist's argument/claim?

Identify proof in the text that supports the author's/scientist's argument/claim.

How does the information about _____ (*scientific concept*) help support the author's/scientist's argument/claim?

Why might the author/scientist have included information about _____ (*scientific concept*)?

What other evidence could the author/scientist have included to make his/her argument stronger?

What evidence is there that other scientists agree with _____'s (*author/scientist*) reasoning?

If _____ (*fact*) is true, what conclusions can you draw about _____ (*argument/claim*)?

Name: _____ Date: _____

Grasslands

Directions: Read this text, and answer the questions.

The grassland is a biome found in areas with hot, dry summers and mild, wet winters. This environment can be found in parts of the United States, Mexico, and Chile and in much of Australia and South Africa. Grasslands cover one-fourth of Earth's land. Every continent has them, except for Antarctica.

In Africa, zebras and giraffes graze on the grasslands. Buffalo once lived on the North American plains, or grasslands. Now, sheep and cattle have replaced them. All over the world, people have turned grasslands into farms to grow grain.

Grasslands have evergreen bushes that never grow over 10 feet tall. In some places, these shrubs grow so close together that it's hard to pass through the area.

It does not rain often in grasslands. Lightning strikes can start wildfires that rage across the land. Fires happen often. In fact, the plants depend on them. Fires clear the area and release minerals back into the soil. After a fire, seeds quickly sprout. Grass can sprout from its root system, so it starts to grow again soon after a fire.

1. Identify proof in the text that supports the author's claim that the summers are hot and dry.

   _____

   _____

   _____

2. What reasons does the text provide to support the claim that plants depend on wildfires?

   _____

   _____

   _____

Evaluating Scientific Arguments and Reasoning Question Stems

Use these question stems to develop your own questions for students.

Identify which facts the author uses that best support _____ (*scientific concept*).

Identify the strongest piece of evidence that supports the author's/scientist's reasoning.

Identify the reasons the text provides to support _____ (*argument/claim*).

Explain how the information in sentence/paragraph _____ supports the author's/scientist's argument/claim.

Use specific examples from the text to identify evidence that supports the author's/scientist's argument/claim.

Cite specific examples of how the information about _____ (*scientific concept*) helps support the author's/scientist's argument/claim.

Evaluate why the author/scientist included information about _____ (*scientific concept*). What value does it add to the text?

Identify other evidence the author/scientist could have included to improve his/her argument.

Evaluate whether there are other scientists who agree with _____'s (*author/scientist*) reasoning. Why do/don't they agree?

Give examples of conclusions that can be drawn about _____ (*argument/claim*) if _____ (*fact*) is true.

Name: _____ Date: _____

Water Biomes

Directions: Read this text, and answer the questions.

Riparian Biomes

Many animals can only drink freshwater, not saltwater. Although Earth is mostly covered by water, only three percent of it is fresh, and a majority of that is trapped in polar ice. Therefore, riparian biomes such as rivers, lakes, and estuaries are precious because they have running freshwater. They support a variety of wildlife, including fish, ducks, frogs, and turtles as well as cattails and water plants. Wetlands such as bogs with soggy soil and marshes that have standing water for part of the year are also riparian biomes. Wetlands are important because they store water and stop floods. Some plants and animals, such as salamanders and alligators, live only in wetlands. Despite this, people have drained or filled in thousands of acres of wetlands in order to build homes, farms, and businesses.

Pelagic Biomes

Saltwater covers almost 75 percent of Earth. Oceans, tide pools, and coral reefs, which contain saltwater, are all types of pelagic biomes. These biomes support a variety of life, from microscopic plants and animals to the blue whale, which is the largest animal on Earth. Marine algae supply much of the world's oxygen and absorb enormous amounts of carbon dioxide.

Coral reefs are colorful biomes found in warm, shallow parts of the ocean. One out of every four pelagic species makes its home there! But coral reefs are sensitive to water temperature. Global warming has heated the seawater. If it doesn't cool down, all coral reefs will die within 50 years.

1. Identify the reasons the text provides to support the idea that riparian biomes are precious.

_____

_____

_____

2. Evaluate why the author included information about the draining of wetlands to build homes, farms, and businesses. What value does it add to the text?

_____

_____

_____

Evaluating Scientific Arguments and Reasoning K–12 Alignment

Use this chart to determine the best question stems for your different groups of students.

★	●	■	▲
What facts tell about _____ (*scientific concept*)?	What facts does the author use to support _____ (*scientific concept*)?	How does the author use facts to support _____ (*scientific concept*)?	Identify which facts the author uses that best support _____ (*scientific concept*).
What fact best tells about _____ (*scientific concept*)?	Which facts best support the author's/scientist's reasoning?	What evidence from the text strongly supports the author's/scientist's reasoning?	Identify the strongest piece of evidence that supports the author's/scientist's reasoning.
What reasons does the text give for _____ (*argument/claim*)?	What reasons are given for _____ (*argument/claim*)?	What reasons does the text provide to support _____ (*argument/claim*)?	Identify the reasons the text provides to support _____ (*argument/claim*).
What words/sentences explain _____ (*argument/claim*)?	What words/sentences support the author's/scientist's argument/claim?	How does the information in sentence/paragraph _____ support the author's/scientist's argument/claim?	Explain how the information in sentence/paragraph _____ supports the author's/scientist's argument/claim.
What other words/sentences tell about _____ (*argument/claim*)?	What proof is in the text to support the author's/scientist's argument/claim?	Identify proof in the text that supports the author's/scientist's argument/claim?	Use specific examples from the text to identify evidence that supports the author's/scientist's argument/claim.

Evaluating Scientific Arguments and Reasoning K–12 Alignment *(cont.)*

★	●	■	▲
What does _____ (*information/fact*) tell about _____ (*scientific concept*)?	How does the information about _____ (*scientific concept*) support the argument/claim?	How does the information about _____ (*scientific concept*) help support the author's/scientist's argument/claim?	Cite specific examples of how the information about _____ (*scientific concept*) helps support the author's/scientist's argument/claim.
Why does the author say _____ (*information/fact*)?	Why does the author include information about _____ (*scientific concept*)?	Why might the author/scientist have included information about _____ (*scientific concept*)?	Evaluate why the author/scientist included information about _____ (*scientific concept*). What value does it add to the text?
What would you add to the text to make it better?	What else could have been added to improve the text?	What other evidence could the author/scientist have included to make his/her argument stronger?	Identify other evidence the author/scientist could have included to improve his/her argument.
Do others agree with the text? If so, who?	What other scientists agree with _____ (*author/scientist*)?	What evidence is there that other scientists agree with _____'s (*author/scientist*) reasoning?	Evaluate whether there are other scientists who agree with _____'s (*author/scientist*) reasoning. Why do/don't they agree?
If you know _____ (*fact*), what do you know about _____ (*argument/claim*)?	If you know _____ (*fact*), what can you say about _____ (*argument/claim*)?	If _____ (*fact*) is true, what conclusions can you draw about _____ (*argument/claim*)?	Give examples of conclusions that can be drawn about _____ (*argument/claim*) if _____ (*fact*) is true.

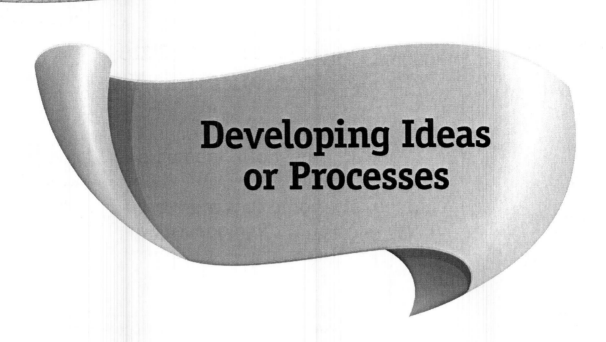

Developing Ideas or Processes

Skill Overview

Explanations of scientific processes are often sequential and require accuracy to obtain reliable data and evidence. The data and evidence can then be used to support conclusions. Explanations of these processes must also include sufficient details so that other scientists can replicate any experimentation. Students should consider authors' or scientists' explanations of scientific processes such as observing, measuring, classifying, sorting, predicting, and inferring.

To develop their awareness of scientific processes, students can consider what might happen if a process were altered or what outcomes might result from a given process. Students may also consider what relationships exist between ideas and processes described in texts.

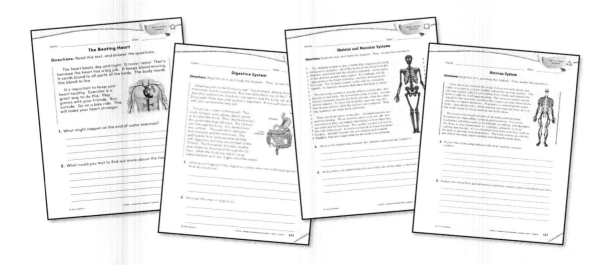

Implementing the Question Stems

This section includes 10 leveled, text-dependent question stems about developing ideas or processes. You can implement these question stems by connecting them to the texts that you are reading in class.

It may seem as though using question stems would be easy, but it can be a complex task for teachers. To help you see how to implement these question stems in your classroom, this section includes student pages containing texts with sample text-dependent questions. Each of the four student pages illustrates a different complexity level.

Snapshot of Differentiating a Question

The chart below models how a single leveled question stem can be tied to science texts at four complexity levels. This snapshot also gives a quick view of how the question stems differ based on the complexity levels. However, you can also see how the question stems link to one another.

	Question Stem	Example
☆	What is the first step in _____ (procedure/process)?	What is the first step in the author's test?
○	What are the steps in _____ (procedure/process)?	What are the steps in the chemical reaction?
▢	Describe the steps in _____ (procedure/process).	Explain the steps in the cloning process.
△	Describe the steps in _____ (procedure/process). What is the significance of the order of the steps?	Describe the steps in the ecological recovery effort. What is the significance of the order of the steps?

Developing Ideas or Processes Question Stems

Use these question stems to develop your own questions for students.

What do you think would happen if _____ (*idea/process*) changed?

What would happen if _____ (*change in scientific concept*)?

Are _____ (*idea/process*) and _____ (*idea/process*) the same? If so, how?

What does the author say is the same about _____ (*idea/process*) and _____ (*idea/process*)?

How are _____ (*idea/process*) and _____ (*idea/process*) the same?

What is the first step in _____ (*procedure/process*)?

What might happen at the end of _____ (*procedure/process*)?

What could you test to find out more about _____ (*scientific concept*)?

Where does the author/scientist predict/observe what will happen/happened?

What patterns do you see in the text?

Name: _____ Date: _____

The Beating Heart

Directions: Read this text, and answer the questions.

The heart beats day and night. It never rests! That's because the heart has a big job. It keeps blood moving. It sends blood to all parts of the body. The body needs this blood to live.

It's important to keep your heart healthy. Exercise is a great way to do this. Play games with your friends. Run outside. Go on a bike ride. This will make your heart stronger.

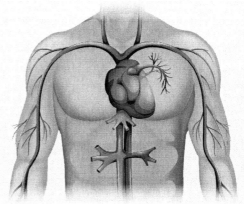

1. What might happen at the end of some exercise?

_____

_____

_____

_____

2. What could you test to find out more about the heart?

_____

_____

_____

_____

_____

Developing Ideas or Processes Question Stems

Use these question stems to develop your own questions for students.

What does the text say would happen if _____ (*idea/process*) changed?

. . . .

What would happen if _____ (*change in scientific concept*)? How do you know?

. . . .

How are _____ (*idea/process*) and _____ (*idea/process*) related?

. . . .

Why does the author compare _____ (*idea/process*) and _____ (*idea/process*)?

. . . .

How are _____ (*idea/process*) and _____ (*idea/process*) the same? How are they different?

. . . .

What are the steps in _____ (*procedure/process*)?

. . . .

What is the outcome of _____ (*procedure/process*)?

. . . .

What experiment could you do to find out more about _____ (*scientific concept*)?

. . . .

Where in the text does the author/scientist describe a prediction/observation?

. . . .

What patterns are described in the text?

Name: _____ Date: _____

Digestive System

Directions: Read this text, and study the diagram. Then, answer the questions.

What happens to the food you eat? You probably already know that it becomes fuel for your body. But how does the body do this? The digestive system turns food into substances that the body can absorb. Every part of the digestive system is important. If one part does not work well, you can become very sick.

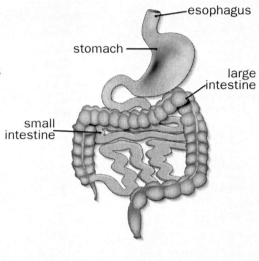

The process starts in the mouth. The teeth, tongue, and salivary glands grind and soften the food. Then, the food enters the gastrointestinal (GI) tract. The GI tract runs through the body. It is divided into two sections. They are the esophagus and stomach, and the intestines. The gallbladder, liver, and pancreas all help with digestion, but they are not part of the GI tract. The food parts become smaller and smaller as they travel through the GI tract. When the body has taken out as many nutrients as it can, it gets rid of the waste.

1. What would happen if the digestive system were not working properly? How do you know?

   _____

   _____

   _____

2. What are the steps in digestion?

   _____

   _____

   _____

LOW   HIGH

Developing Ideas or Processes Question Stems

Use these question stems to develop your own questions for students.

Based on paragraph _____, what would happen if _____ (*idea/process*) changed?

Based on what you read in paragraph _____, what would most likely happen if _____ (*change in concept*)?

What is the relationship between _____ (*idea/process*) and _____ (*idea/process*)?

Where does the author compare _____ (*idea/process*) and _____ (*idea/process*)? Why does the author make this comparison?

What are some similarities between _____ (*idea/process*) and _____ (*idea/process*)? What are some differences?

Describe the steps in _____ (*procedure/process*) in order.

What outcome would result at the end of _____ (*procedure/process*)?

To conduct an experiment on _____ (*concept*), what kind of data would you need to collect?

Where in the text does the author/scientist describe a prediction/observation? Why does the author include it?

What patterns or relationships do you notice about the ideas in the text?

Name: _____ Date: _____

Skeletal and Muscular Systems

Directions: Read this text, and study the diagram. Then, answer the questions.

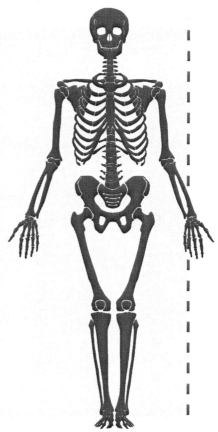

The skeletal system is like a frame that supports the body and gives it structure. All of the bones in the body form the skeleton, and joints link the skeleton together. Some parts of the skeleton protect vital organs. For example, the rib cage protects the heart and lungs, and the skull protects the brain. The skeletal system works with the muscular system. It supports muscles that allow the body to move.

The muscular system is exactly what it sounds like—the muscles in the body. Most muscles come in pairs. As one muscle contracts, it pulls the body one way while the other muscle relaxes. To move the body the opposite way, the first muscle relaxes while the second one contracts. That way, a person can move back and forth.

There are three types of muscles. Skeletal muscles are used for moving. These muscles allow us to run, lift, and exercise, but they can fatigue depending on how often they are used and for how long. The cardiac muscle is found in the wall of the heart. It works constantly to keep the heart beating. Smooth muscles let you swallow and breathe. Together, they are responsible for the body's movements.

1. What is the relationship between the skeletal and muscular systems?

_____

_____

_____

2. What patterns or relationships do you notice about the ideas in the text?

_____

_____

_____

LOW   HIGH

Developing Ideas or Processes Question Stems

Use these question stems to develop your own questions for students.

Based on paragraph _____, predict what would happen if _____ (*idea/process*) changed. Include evidence from the text to support your prediction.

Based on what you read in paragraph _____, predict the outcome if _____ (*change in scientific concept*).

Explain the relationship between _____ (*idea/process*) and _____ (*idea/process*).

Identify the science ideas/processes the author compares, and explain why the comparisons are made.

Analyze the similarities and differences between _____ (*idea/process*) and _____ (*idea/process*).

Describe the steps in _____ (*procedure/process*). What is the significance of the order of the steps?

Describe the results at the end of _____ (*procedure/process*) and how the preceding steps affect them.

Explain what data you would need to collect to conduct an experiment on _____ (*scientific concept*).

For what reasons does the author/scientist describe his/her predictions/observations? What value does it add to the text?

Analyze the patterns or relationships among the scientific ideas in the text.

Name: _____ Date: _____

Nervous System

Directions: Read this text, and study the diagram. Then, answer the questions.

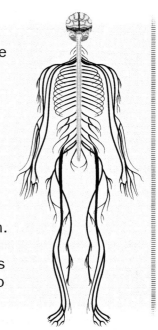

While the brain controls the body, it does not work alone, but rather it is part of a larger system called the nervous system. The nervous system gathers information from inside and outside the body in order to react appropriately. The nervous system sends signals to the muscles, monitors the organs, reviews information, and then it makes decisions. It assists in controlling the entire body. Specialized cells called neurons carry signals from all over the body; however, most neurons are in the brain.

The brain is the most complex of all body parts because it controls so many other systems and functions. It controls involuntary activities such as heartbeats, breathing, and digestion. The brain is also responsible for voluntary activities such as walking and moving. It even handles conscious activities, such as thought, reasoning, and abstraction. The brain makes up only two percent of the body, but it controls everything the body does.

1. Explain the relationship between the brain and the nervous system.

_____

_____

_____

_____

2. Analyze the similarities and differences between voluntary and involuntarily activities.

_____

_____

_____

_____

Developing Ideas or Processes
K–12 Alignment

Use this chart to determine the best question stems for your different groups of students.

★	●	■	▲
What do you think would happen if _____ (*idea/process*) changed?	What does the text say would happen if _____ (*idea/process*) changed?	Based on paragraph _____, what would happen if _____ (*idea/process*) changed?	Based on paragraph _____, predict what would happen if _____ (*idea/process*) changed. Include evidence from the text to support your prediction.
What would happen if _____ (*change in scientific concept*)?	What would happen if _____ (*change in scientific concept*)? How do you know?	Based on what you read in paragraph _____, what would most likely happen if _____ (*change in scientific concept*)?	Based on what you read in paragraph _____, predict the outcome if _____ (*change in scientific concept*).
Are _____ (*idea/process*) and _____ (*idea/process*) the same? If so, how?	How are _____ (*idea/process*) and _____ (*idea/process*) related?	What is the relationship between _____ (*idea/process*) and _____ (*idea/process*)?	Explain the relationship between _____ (*idea/process*) and _____ (*idea/process*).
What does the author say is the same about _____ (*idea/process*) and _____ (*idea/process*)?	Why does the author compare _____ (*idea/process*) and _____ (*idea/process*)?	Where does the author compare _____ (*idea/process*) and _____ (*idea/process*)? Why does the author make this comparison?	Identify the scientific ideas/processes the author compares, and explain why the comparisons are made.
How are _____ (*idea/process*) and _____ (*idea/process*) the same?	How are _____ (*idea/process*) and _____ (*idea/process*) the same? How are they different?	What are some similarities between _____ (*idea/process*) and _____ (*idea/process*)? What are some differences?	Analyze the similarities and differences between _____ (*idea/process*) and _____ (*idea/process*).

Developing Ideas or Processes
K–12 Alignment *(cont.)*

★	●	■	▲
What is the first step in _____ (*procedure/process*)?	What are the steps in _____ (*procedure/process*)?	Describe the steps in _____ (*procedure/process*) in order.	Describe the steps in _____ (*procedure/process*). What is the significance of the order of the steps?
What might happen at the end of _____ (*procedure/process*)?	What is the outcome of _____ (*procedure/process*)?	What outcome would result at the end of _____ (*procedure/process*)?	Describe the results at the end of _____ (*procedure/process*) and how the preceding steps affect them.
What could you test to find out more about _____ (*scientific concept*)?	What experiment could you do to find out more about _____ (*scientific concept*)?	To conduct an experiment on _____ (*scientific concept*), what kind of data would you need to collect?	Explain what data you would need to collect to conduct an experiment on _____ (*scientific concept*).
Where does the author/scientist predict/observe what will happen/happened?	Where in the text does the author/scientist describe a prediction/observation?	Where in the text does the author/scientist describe a prediction/observation? Why does the author include it?	For what reasons does the author/scientist describe his/her predictions/observations? What value does it add to the text?
What patterns do you see in the text?	What patterns are described in the text?	What patterns or relationships do you notice about the ideas in the text?	Analyze the patterns or relationships among the scientific ideas in the text.

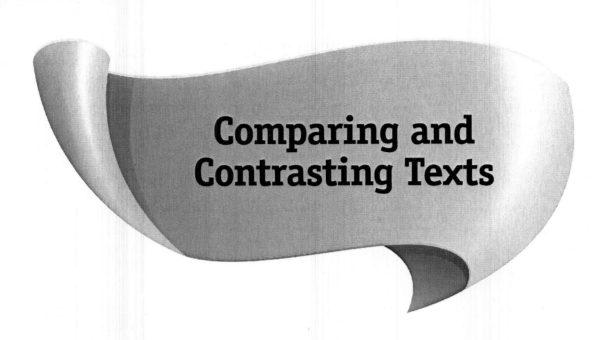

Comparing and Contrasting Texts

Skill Overview

Science requires authors to combine reliable information and data from multiple sources to develop working understandings of different concepts. Students learning to read scientific texts must also learn to analyze multiple sources of information to develop solid understandings of processes and concepts. Teaching students how to compare and contrast texts can increase students' comprehension of the concepts and can improve their higher-order thinking skills.

Students should learn to identify similarities and differences between the content, text structures, purposes, and text features of various scientific texts. To do this, students will need time to develop their understandings of individual texts separately before attempting to compare and contrast them.

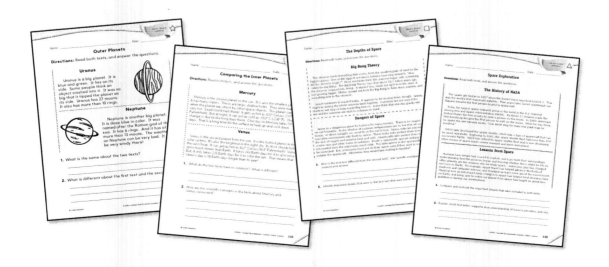

Implementing the Question Stems

This section includes 10 leveled, text-dependent question stems about comparing and contrasting texts. You can implement these question stems by connecting them to the texts that you are reading in class.

It may seem as though using question stems would be easy, but it can be a complex task for teachers. To help you see how to implement these question stems in your classroom, this section includes student pages containing texts with sample text-dependent questions. Each of the four student pages illustrates a different complexity level.

Snapshot of Differentiating a Question

The chart below models how a single leveled question stem can be tied to science texts at four complexity levels. This snapshot also gives a quick view of how the question stems differ based on the complexity levels. However, you can also see how the question stems link to one another.

	Question Stem	Example
☆	What did you learn about _____ (scientific concept) when you read the texts?	What did you learn about seeds when you read the texts?
○	What conclusion can you draw about _____ (scientific concept) by comparing the texts?	What conclusion can you draw about pollination by comparing the texts?
□	What key conclusion about _____ (scientific concept) can be made by comparing the two texts?	What key conclusion about plant reproduction can be made by comparing the two texts?
△	Describe any scientific conclusions that can be made by comparing the two texts.	Describe any scientific conclusions that can be made by comparing the two texts on angiosperm and gymnosperm reproduction.

Comparing and Contrasting Texts Question Stems

Use these question stems to develop your own questions for students.

What do _____ (*text A*) and _____ (*text B*) have in common?

What is the same about the two texts?

What does _____ (*scientific concept in text A*) have to do with _____ (*scientific concept in text B*)?

What did you learn about _____ (*scientific concept*) when you read the texts?

Do the two texts tell about the same things? If so, what?

What is different about _____ (*text A*) and _____ (*text B*)?

What did you learn in _____ (*text A*) that was not in _____ (*text B*)?

Which text helps you learn about _____ (*scientific concept*) the best? Why?

What do _____ (*text A*) and _____ (*text B*) have to do with each other?

Which text best tells about _____ (*scientific concept*)? Why?

Name: _____   Date: _____

Outer Planets

Directions: Read both texts, and answer the questions.

Uranus

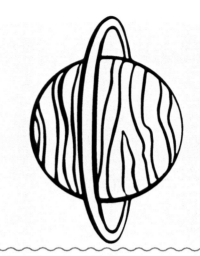

Uranus is a big planet. It is blue and green. It lies on its side. Some people think an object crashed into it. It was so big that it tipped the planet on its side. Uranus has 27 moons. It also has more than 10 rings.

Neptune

Neptune is another big planet. It is deep blue in color. It was named after the Roman god of the sea. It has 6 rings. And it has at more than 13 moons. The weather on Neptune can be very bad. It can be very windy there!

1. What is the same about the two texts?

_____

_____

2. What is different about the first text and the second text?

_____

_____

_____

Comparing and Contrasting Texts Question Stems

Use these question stems to develop your own questions for students.

How is _____ (*text A*) similar to _____ (*text B*)?

What do the two texts have in common? What is different?

How are _____ (*scientific concept in text A*) and _____ (*scientific concept in text B*) connected?

What conclusion can you draw about _____ (*scientific concept*) by comparing the texts?

Do the two texts seem to agree or disagree on the cause/effect/ impact of _____ (*scientific concept*)? How do you know?

How do the authors describe/explain _____ (*scientific concept*) differently?

What important details were in _____ (*text A*) that were not in _____ (*text B*)?

Which text helps you understand _____ (*scientific concept*) better? Why?

How are the scientific concepts in _____ (*text A*) and _____ (*text B*) connected?

Which text best explains _____ (*scientific concept*)? Use details to explain why?

Name: _____ Date: _____

Comparing the Inner Planets

Directions: Read both texts, and answer the questions.

Mercury

Mercury is the closest planet to the sun. It is also the smallest planet. It has many craters. These are large, shallow holes. They were made when the planet was struck by other space objects. The planet can get very hot. Lead could melt there! It gets as hot as 425° Celsius (797° Fahrenheit). But at night, it can get as cold as -150° C (-238° F). The big change is due to the long days there. One day on Mercury takes 59 Earth days. That is a long time for the surface to heat up and cool down.

Venus

Venus is the second planet from the sun. It is the hottest planet in the solar system. It's also the brightest in the night sky. Its thick clouds hold the sun's heat. It can get as hot as 462° Celsius (864° Fahrenheit)! Venus spins much slower than Earth. It takes 243 Earth days for it to spin once. But, it only takes 225 Earth days for it to orbit the sun. That means that Venus's day is 18 Earth days longer than its year!

1. What do the two texts have in common? What is different?

   _____

   _____

2. How are the scientific concepts in the texts about Mercury and Venus connected?

   _____

   _____

   _____

Comparing and Contrasting Texts Question Stems

Use these question stems to develop your own questions for students.

How is _____ (*text A*) similar to/different from _____ (*text B*)? Use specific examples to support your answer.

How are the ideas in the two texts the same? How are the ideas different?

Explain how _____ (*scientific concept in text A*) and _____ (*scientific concept in text A*) are related.

What key conclusion about _____ (*scientific concept*) can be made by comparing the two texts?

Are the two texts in agreement on the cause/effect/impact of _____ (*scientific concept*)? Provide evidence to support your answer.

How do the authors describe/explain _____ (*scientific concept*) differently? Include examples from the texts to show the differences.

Identify important details that were in _____ (*text A*) that were not in _____ (*text B*).

Which text gives you the most support for understanding _____ (*scientific concept*)? Why?

What is the relationship between the scientific concepts in _____ (*text A*) and _____ (*text B*)?

Which text provides a clearer explanation of _____ (*scientific concept*)? Include evidence to support your reasoning.

Name: _____ Date: _____

The Depths of Space

Directions: Read both texts, and answer the questions.

Big Bang Theory

The universe holds everything that exists, from the smallest grain of sand to the biggest galaxy. One of the biggest questions humans have long asked is, "How did the universe begin?" Most scientists think the universe began with something called the Big Bang. The Big Bang Theory says that about 13.7 billion years ago, the universe snapped into being. It started very small, but right from the start, it was growing bigger. Matter spread out from the Big Bang to form stars, planets, and everything else in the universe.

Space continues to expand today. It appears to be slowing down, though. Gravity might be pulling the whole universe back together. Scientists are not sure if the universe will stop or keep expanding forever. Some think that one day, gravity will win and the universe will start to collapse on itself.

Dangers of Space

Space is a dangerous place for humans for many reasons. There is no oxygen, so we can't breathe. In the shadow of a planet, temperatures are so low that we would freeze. In direct sunlight, we would fry in the sun's heat. Space suits let astronauts take their environment with them to space. These bulky suits protect them from the lack of oxygen and extreme heat and cold. Spacecrafts also protect them from cosmic rays and other forms of radiation. Inside a spacecraft, special clothing is not needed once the astronauts reach orbit. The atmosphere in the spacecraft can be controlled. But, astronauts must put on their space suits if they want to work outside the spacecraft. Otherwise, they would have nothing to breathe!

1. How is the first text different from the second text? Use specific examples to support your answer.

   _____

   _____

2. Identify important details that were in the first text that were not in the second text.

   _____

   _____

Comparing and Contrasting Texts Question Stems

Use these question stems to develop your own questions for students.

Compare and contrast the two texts, using specific examples to support your response.

Outline the key ideas of each text. Which ideas are similar, and which are different?

Use specific examples to explain the ways _____ (*scientific concept in text A*) and _____ (*scientific concept in text B*) are related.

Describe any scientific conclusions that can be made by comparing the two texts.

Use evidence from the texts to analyze whether they both agree on the cause/effect/impact of _____ (*scientific concept*).

Use examples from the texts to describe the differences in how the authors describe/explain _____ (*scientific concept*).

Compare and contrast the important details that were included in both texts.

Explain which text better supports your understanding of _____ (*scientific concept*), and why.

Analyze and describe the relationships between the scientific concepts in _____ (*text A*) and _____ (*text B*).

Use textual evidence to determine which text provides the clearest explanation of _____ (*scientific concept*), and why.

Name: _____ Date: _____

Space Exploration

Directions: Read both texts, and answer the questions.

The History of NASA

The space age began in 1957 when the Soviet Union launched *Sputnik 1*. This was the world's first man-made satellite. Four years later, Soviet cosmonaut Yuri Gagarin became the first person to pilot a spacecraft.

Today, the largest space research group in the world is the U.S. National Aeronautics and Space Administration (NASA). Its *Apollo 11* mission made the United States the first country to land a person on the moon. In 1969, astronaut Neil Armstrong became the first person to walk on the moon. While he was there, he spoke the now famous words, "One small step for man; one giant leap for mankind."

NASA later developed the space shuttle, which was a type of spacecraft that can be used repeatedly. Beginning in 1981, the space shuttle fleet had more than 100 successful flights. NASA has retired its space shuttle fleet and is now developing other means of space travel—some manned and some unmanned.

Lessons from Space

Humans have always had a need to explore and learn from their surroundings. Understanding how the universe began and learning whether there might be life on other planets are two reasons why we study space. Astronomy also has changed our lives on Earth. For example, space travel has helped advance the fields of medicine and computer science, and it helped us learn more about the environment. Studying how an astronaut's body changes in space has helped treat diseases here on Earth, and being able to watch our planet from space has taught us about how pollution is hurting our environment.

1. Compare and contrast the important details that were included in both texts.

   _____

   _____

2. Explain which text better supports your understanding of travel exploration, and why.

   _____

   _____

Comparing and Contrasting Texts
K–12 Alignment

Use this chart to determine the best question stems for your different groups of students.

★	●	■	▲
What do _____ (*text A*) and _____ (*text B*) have in common?	How is _____ (*text A*) similar to _____ (*text B*)?	How is _____ (*text A*) similar to/different from _____ (*text B*)? Use specific examples to support your answer.	Compare and contrast the two texts, using specific examples to support your response.
What is the same about the two texts?	What do the two texts have in common? What is different?	How are the ideas in the two texts the same? How are the ideas different?	Outline the key ideas of each text. Which ideas are similar, and which are different?
What does _____ (*scientific concept in text A*) have to do with _____ (*scientific concept in text B*)?	How are _____ (*scientific concept in text A*) and _____ (*scientific concept in text B*) connected?	Explain how _____ (*scientific concept in text A*) and _____ (*scientific concept in text*) B are related.	Use specific examples to explain the ways _____ (*scientific concept in text A*) and _____ (*scientific concept in text B*) are related.
What did you learn about _____ (*scientific concept*) when you read the texts?	What conclusion can you draw about _____ (*scientific concept*) by comparing the texts?	What key conclusion about _____ (*scientific concept*) can be made by comparing the two texts?	Describe any scientific conclusions that can be made by comparing the two texts.
Do the two texts tell about the same things? If so, what?	Do the two texts seem to agree or disagree on the cause/effect/ impact of _____ (*scientific concept*)? How do you know?	Are the two texts in agreement on the cause/effect/impact of _____ (*scientific concept*)? Provide evidence to support your answer.	Use evidence from the texts to analyze whether they both agree on the cause/effect/impact of _____ (*scientific concept*).

Comparing and Contrasting Texts
K–12 Alignment *(cont.)*

★	●	■	▲
What is different about _____ (*text A*) and _____ (*text B*)?	How do the authors describe/explain _____ (*scientific concept*) differently?	How do the authors describe/explain _____ (*scientific concept*) differently? Include examples from the texts to show the differences.	Use examples from the texts to describe the differences in how the authors describe/explain _____ (*scientific concept*).
What did you learn in _____ (*text A*) that was not in _____ (*text B*)?	What important details were in _____ (*text A*) that were not in _____ (*text B*)?	Identify important details that were in _____ (*text A*) that were not in _____ (*text B*).	Compare and contrast the important details that were included in both texts.
Which text helps you learn about _____ (*scientific concept*) the best? Why?	Which text helps you understand _____ (*scientific concept*) better? Why?	Which text gives you the most support for understanding _____ (*scientific concept*)? Why?	Explain which text better supports your understanding of _____ (*scientific concept*), and why.
What do _____ (*text A*) and _____ (*text B*) have to do with each other?	How are the scientific concepts in _____ (*text A*) and _____ (*text B*) connected?	What is the relationship between the scientific concepts in _____ (*text A*) and _____ (*text B*)?	Analyze and describe the relationship between the scientific concepts in _____ (*text A*) and _____ (*text B*).
Which text best tells about _____ (*scientific concept*)? Why?	Which text best explains _____ (*scientific concept*)? Use details to explain why.	Which text provides a clearer explanation of _____ (*scientific concept*)? Include evidence to support your reasoning.	Use textual evidence to determine which text provides the clearest explanation of _____ (*scientific concept*), and why.

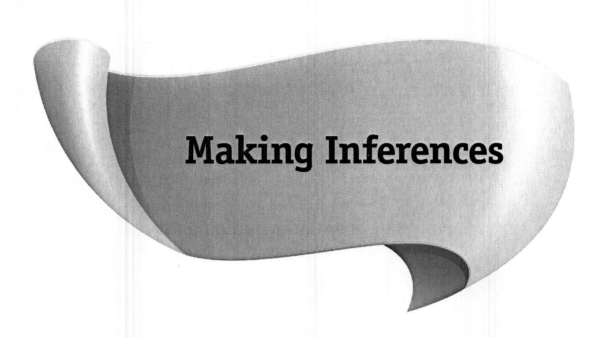

Making Inferences

Skill Overview

A scientific inference is a conclusion drawn from evidence and logical reasoning. Scientists might investigate concepts that they cannot directly observe or measure. Instead, they collect evidence and then make reasoned inferences to explain concepts. The more evidence they collect, the more confident they can become that their inferences are correct.

Similarly, authors do not always directly explain the connections between concepts presented in texts. Readers must look for evidence that will allow them to identify these connections. The more evidence they can find in texts, the more confident they can become in their inferences. Making these inferential connections is necessary for students to fully understand complex scientific texts.

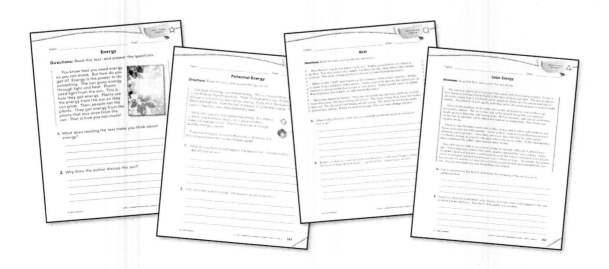

Implementing the Question Stems

This section includes 10 leveled, text-dependent question stems about making inferences. You can implement these question stems by connecting them to the texts that you are reading in class.

It may seem as though using question stems would be easy, but it can be a complex task for teachers. To help you see how to implement these question stems in your classroom, this section includes student pages containing texts with sample text-dependent questions. Each of the four student pages illustrates a different complexity level.

Snapshot of Differentiating a Question

The chart below models how a single leveled question stem can be tied to science texts at four complexity levels. This snapshot also gives a quick view of how the question stems differ based on the complexity levels. However, you can also see how the question stems link to one another.

	Question Stem	Example
☆	What did you learn from the chart/graph/image?	What did you learn about animals from the chart?
◯	What information can you find about _____ (scientific concept) from the chart/graph/image?	What information can you find about animal cells from the image?
▢	Based on the information in the chart/graph/image, what can you infer about _____ (scientific concept)?	Based on the information in the graph, what can you infer about forces and motion?
△	Use details to explain what you can infer from the chart/graph/image about _____ (scientific concept).	Use details to explain what you can infer from the chart about the effect of gravity on the object.

Making Inferences Question Stems

Use these question stems to develop your own questions for students.

What did you learn from the chart/graph/image?

What does reading the text make you think about _____ (*scientific concept*)?

What might the author tell about next?

What does the author think about _____ (*scientific concept*)?

What would be different if _____ (*part of scientific concept*) changed?

What would happen if _____ (*process*) stopped/reversed/slowed down/sped up?

What do you think _____ (*word/phrase*) means?

What would happen if _____ (*step*) were left out?

What do you think happened? How do you know?

Why does the author discuss _____ (*scientific concept*)?

Name: _____ Date: _____

Energy

Directions: Read this text, and answer the questions.

You know that you need energy so you can move. But how do you get it? Energy is the power to do something. The sun gives energy through light and heat. Plants need light from the sun. This is how they get energy. Plants use the energy from the sun so they can grow. Then, people eat the plants. They get energy from the plants that was once from the sun. That is how you can move!

1. What does reading the text make you think about energy?

    _____

    _____

    _____

    _____

2. Why does the author discuss the sun?

    _____

    _____

    _____

    _____

Making Inferences Question Stems

Use these question stems to develop your own questions for students.

What information can you find about _____ (*scientific concept*) from the chart/graph/image?

What conclusion can you draw about _____ (*scientific concept*)?

What do you think the author might explain next? Why?

What is the author's opinion about _____ (*scientific concept*)?

What do you think would happen if _____ (*part of scientific concept*) changed?

What would happen if _____ (*process*) stopped/reversed/slowed down/sped up? Use the text to support your answer.

After reading paragraph _____, what do you think _____ (*word/ phrase*) means?

If _____ (*step*) were left out of the process/procedure, what might happen?

What do the data/observations suggest? How do you know?

Why does the author include information about _____ (*scientific concept*)?

Name: _____ Date: _____

Potential Energy

Directions: Read this text, and answer the questions.

One type of energy is potential energy. This is stored energy. It can come from an object's position. Think of a ball at the top of a hill. Even though it isn't moving, the ball has energy. If you let it, the ball will move. When the ball rolls down the hill, it releases its potential energy. The same is true for water stored behind a dam.

Molecules can also have potential energy. It is stored in the bonds between atoms. It is released when chemical changes occur. The bonds break or change, and the energy is spent.

Potential energy is stored in the nucleus of atoms, too. It is released when the nucleus breaks apart.

1. What do you think would happen if a dam broke? Use the text to support your answer.

    _____

    _____

    _____

    _____

2. Why does the author include information about molecules?

    _____

    _____

    _____

    _____

COMPLEXITY

LOW ⭐ ● ▢ ▲ HIGH

Making Inferences Question Stems

Use these question stems to develop your own questions for students.

Based on the information in the chart/graph/image, what can you infer about _____ (*scientific concept*)?

After reading this text, what can you conclude about _____ (*scientific concept*)?

After reading the text, what is the author likely to explain next? How do you know?

What is the author's opinion about _____ (*scientific concept*)? How do you know?

What would happen if _____ (*part of scientific concept*) changed? Use information from the text to support your answer.

Based on what you read about _____ (*process*), what would happen if this stopped/reversed/slowed down/sped up? Use the text to support your answer.

How can you use the text to determine the meaning of _____ (*word/phrase*) in paragraph _____?

Use the text to infer what would happen if _____ (*step*) were left out of the process/procedure.

What can you conclude based on the data/observations in this text?

Why does the author include information about _____ (*scientific concept*)? How does it affect the text?

Name: _____ Date: _____

Heat

Directions: Read this text, and answer the questions.

Heat doesn't stay in one place—it moves. It gets passed from one object to another. This may sound very simple, but there are big ideas behind this simple concept. The study of heat and how it moves is called thermodynamics.

Matter is the "stuff" that makes up the contents of the entire universe. Matter is made of tiny particles called atoms. Atoms cannot be seen by the naked eye—it requires a very powerful microscope to see atoms. Atoms are the basis of matter. How they move has a lot to do with thermodynamics.

Atoms are always in motion. They are constantly moving back and forth, and the more they move, the more energy they have. The more energy they have, the hotter they are. The atoms in cold things vibrate slowly. The atoms in hot things move around very quickly. If they move fast enough, they can even change phases.

1. After reading the text, what can you conclude about the atoms in a bowl of hot soup?

    _____

    _____

    _____

    _____

2. Based on what you read about thermodynamics, what would happen if the atoms in the bowl of soup slowed down? Use the text to support your answer.

    _____

    _____

    _____

    _____

Making Inferences Question Stems

Use these question stems to develop your own questions for students.

Use details to explain what you can infer from the chart/graph/image about _____ (*scientific concept*).

Use examples from the text to describe what you can conclude about _____ (*scientific concept*).

Use the information from the text to predict what the author might explain next.

What details from the text help you determine the author's opinion about _____ (*scientific concept*)?

Predict what would happen if _____ (*part of scientific concept*) changed. Justify your prediction using information from the text.

Based on what you read about _____ (*process*), describe what would happen if this stopped/reversed/slowed down/sped up. Use the text to justify your answer.

Use evidence from the text to determine the meaning of _____ (*word/phrase*) in paragraph _____.

Use textual evidence to infer what would happen if _____ (*step*) were left out of the process/procedure.

What can you conclude from the data/observations in this text? Support you answer with textual evidence.

Cite specific examples from the text that help you understand why information about _____ (*scientific concept*) is included.

Name: _____ Date: _____

Solar Energy

Directions: Read this text, and answer the questions.

The sun is a giant ball of incredibly hot gases with tremendous energy. Some of this energy is transported to Earth in the form of heat and light. The sun produces so much energy that it constantly emits photons, which are minuscule packets of energy. The photons travel rapidly until they arrive at various places on planet Earth.

Some of the photons hit air molecules in the atmosphere, making those air molecules warmer. The air on the side of the planet facing the sun naturally heats up more than the side facing away. Hot air expands and cold air contracts, so the hot air spreads out to where the cold air is contracting. This movement creates winds.

Photons also hit water molecules in the oceans and in other water bodies, and those molecules become warmer. Some of them heat so much that they become gaseous and evaporate. Since they are warm, they rise into the atmosphere, eventually arriving at a higher elevation where the air is colder. In the atmosphere, they condense into water vapor and become clouds.

Even the car you ride in uses solar energy to operate, although it arrived eons ago. When dinosaurs walked the earth, plants captured the sun's energy. When the plants died and became buried underground, the energy remained in the plants, which were squeezed and compressed over millions of years. Eventually, the plants turned into oil, and the oil was converted into gasoline that gets pumped into your car. So, you can thank the sun for getting you around.

1. Use evidence from the text to determine the meaning of the word *solar* in paragraph four.

   _____

   _____

   _____

2. Based on what you read about solar energy, describe what would happen if the sun produced fewer photons. Use the text to justify your answer.

   _____

   _____

   _____

   _____

Making Inferences K–12 Alignment

Use this chart to determine the best question stems for your different groups of students.

★	●	■	▲
What did you learn from the chart/graph/image?	What information can you find about _____ (*scientific concept*) from the chart/graph/image?	Based on the information in the chart/graph/image, what can you infer about _____ (*scientific concept*)?	Use details to explain what you can infer from the chart/graph/image about _____ (*scientific concept*).
What does reading the text make you think about _____ (*scientific concept*)?	What conclusion can you draw about _____ (*scientific concept*)?	After reading this text, what can you conclude about _____ (*scientific concept*)?	Use examples from the text to describe what you can conclude about _____ (*scientific concept*).
What might the author tell about next?	What do you think the author might explain next? Why?	After reading the text, what is the author likely to explain next? How do you know?	Use the information from the text to predict what the author might explain next.
What does the author think about _____ (*scientific concept*)?	What is the author's opinion about _____ (*scientific concept*)?	What is the author's opinion about _____ (*scientific concept*)? How do you know?	What details from the text help you determine the author's opinion about _____ (*scientific concept*)?
What would be different if _____ (*part of scientific concept*) changed?	What do you think would happen if _____ (*part of scientific concept*) changed?	What would happen if _____ (*part of scientific concept*) changed? Use information from the text to support your answer.	Predict what would happen if _____ (*part of scientific concept*) changed. Justify your prediction using information from the text.

Making Inferences K–12 Alignment (cont.)

★	●	■	▲
What would happen if _____ (process) stopped/reversed/slowed down/sped up?	What would happen if _____ (process) stopped/reversed/slowed down/sped up? Use the text to support your answer.	Based on what you read about _____ (process), what would happen if this stopped/reversed/slowed down/sped up? Use the text to support your answer.	Based on what you read about _____ (process), describe what would happen if this stopped/reversed/slowed down/sped up. Use the text to justify your answer.
What do you think _____ (word/phrase) means?	After reading paragraph _____, what do you think _____ (word/phrase) means?	How can you use the text to determine the meaning of _____ (word/phrase) in paragraph _____?	Use evidence from the text to determine the meaning of _____ (word/phrase) in paragraph _____.
What would happen if _____ (step) were left out?	If _____ (step) were left out of the process/procedure, what might happen?	Use the text to infer what would happen if _____ (step) were left out of the process/procedure.	Use textual evidence to infer what would happen if _____ (step) were left out of the process/procedure.
What do you think happened? How do you know?	What do the data/observations suggest? How do you know?	What can you conclude based on the data/observations in this text?	What can you conclude from the data/observations in this text? Support your answer with textual evidence.
Why does the author discuss_____ (scientific concept)?	Why does the author include information about _____ (scientific concept)?	Why does the author include information about _____ (scientific concept)? How does it affect the text?	Cite specific examples from the text that help you understand why information about _____ (scientific concept) is included.

Answer Key

Answers will vary. Possible answers and sample answers are provided.

Animal Needs (page 13)

1. The text is about the things animals need to survive.

2. Words include: *food*, *air*, and *water*.

Worms (page 15)

1. The scientific concept is that worms are simple animals that play an important role in farming. Sentences that tell this include: "They don't even have brains!" and "They make the soil better for growing crops."

2. Example: Worms: Big Eaters. This is appropriate because the text says that all worms do is eat.

Echinoderms (page 17)

1. Example: Symmetry in the Ocean. This is supported by the text because Echinoderms live in the ocean and have symmetry.

2. The author describes radial symmetry as when an animal has many identical parts. The author compares radial symmetry to the spokes on a wheel.

Types of Animals (page 19)

1. The scientific concept is that organisms are classified by a system of taxonomy. It groups organisms that have similar characteristics. Each successive classification divides into smaller categories.

2. Example: Morphological groupings are not always beneficial because even though animals may have one thing in common, they may not have others in common. The author used the example of ostriches and humans both having two legs but otherwise not being similar.

Leaves (page 25)

1. Example: The list supports the idea that there are many types of leaves.

2. Details include: there are needles on pine trees, there are fronds on palms, and some leaves are soft and hairy, while others are smooth and shiny.

Roots (page 27)

1. Example: Plants have roots to absorb water and nutrients from the soil. The details explain this by telling how nutrients are dissolved in the soil and how plants use the nutrients to grow.

2. Example: The most important detail from paragraph two is that plants use nutrients in the water to grow.

The Sun's Energy (page 29)

1. Plants use energy to grow and to produce more plants by making seeds, flowers, or fruit.

2. The main scientific concept is that the sun provides energy used on Earth. Details that support this include: plants produce oxygen, plants use sunlight to grow and reproduce, animals eat plants for energy, and the sun powers the water cycle.

The World of Plants (page 31)

1. Details include: people consume a wide variety of plants, farmers grow crops in vast amounts, and they supply entire cities of people with food.

2. Example: The most important scientific detail in paragraph one is that many types of animals are dependent on plants. This is significant because plants play an important role in our ecosystem.

Light and Sight (page 37)

1. The sentence "Our eyes see this light" tells about what our eyes see.

2. People don't see objects. We see the light that bounces off objects.

Answer Key (cont.)

Seeing Lights (page 39)

1. The author says that natural light comes from the sun and other stars.

2. Example: The most important ideas are that light is a form of energy, and it travels in waves.

Reflection, Refraction, and Absorption (page 41)

1. Example: The sentence that best summarizes reflection is, "When light is reflected, the light rays bounce off a surface and go in a different direction." This is a good summary because it briefly describes what is detailed in the rest of the paragraph.

2. Example: The main idea of paragraph two is that refraction occurs when light bends as it travels through a transparent material.

The Science of Sound (page 43)

1. Example: The sentence that provides the most succinct summary is, "Sound is created from vibrations of materials." This idea is further explained in the rest of the text.

2. Example: Sound is created by vibrations that pulse through the air. They are then perceived by our ears. Differences in these vibrations make each sound different. The differences include wavelength, amplitude, and frequency.

Cells (page 49)

1. The picture shows that the boy's skin is made up of cells.

2. Example: The picture helps me read the text because I can imagine how small the cells must be because we can't see them.

All About Cells (page 51)

1. The diagram provides a visual of a cell with the cell membrane and nucleus labeled.

2. Example: The author included the diagram to show what a cell looks like and to show where the nucleus and cell membrane are.

Organelles (page 53)

1. Example: The diagram clarifies what each organelle looks like and where it is located.

2. Example: The diagram also shows the reader that plant cells have a cell wall and a cell membrane. It is important because this is part of the cell's structure.

Comparing Organelles (page 55)

1. The diagrams show the organelles in plant and animal cells. They also show that while both plant and animal cells have mitochondria and nuclei, only plant cells have chloroplasts.

Simple Machines (page 61)

1. Example: The author wrote this text to help me understand what simple machines are.

2. Example: The seesaw made me realize that simple machines are everywhere.

Forces (page 63)

1. Example: The author wants me to understand that forces act upon all objects all the time, even when they are not moving.

2. The author's examples help the reader understand the role that forces play on things that move and things that aren't moving.

Newton's Laws of Motion (page 65)

1. Example: The author wants readers to understand what Newton's laws of motion are and what they mean. I know this because the text gives details about each law.

2. The author means that you can feel the chair under your body pushing you up while gravity is pushing you down. Evidence provided includes that the forces are balanced, Newton's opposite reaction, and movement only occurs when forces are unbalanced.

Answer Key (cont.)

Magnets and Electromagnetism (page 67)

1. The author includes this example to show that the magnet has an invisible field. It supports her purpose by proving that her claim is correct.

2. The author means that magnets always have two poles. Evidence includes: wherever there is a north pole, there is a south pole, and if you break a magnet in half, both pieces will have a north and a south pole.

Jet Streams (page 73)

1. *Moisture* means the small amount of liquid in the air.

2. Words include: *rivers of wind, blow very fast, move the moisture around, high in the sky,* and *jet planes.*

Trade Winds (page 75)

1. Words include: *east to west, patterns,* water *vapor, air falling,* and *rotates.*

2. The word *evaporate* helps a reader understand the role that water vapor plays in creating trade winds.

Hurricanes (page 77)

1. Hurricanes gather water from the sea through evaporation. The first paragraph explains this.

2. The scientific meaning of the word *eye* is the low-pressure center of a hurricane where there are no clouds or wind. The everyday meaning is the organ that you see with.

Earthquakes (page 79)

1. Example: Earthquakes occur when the Earth's surface moves and shifts violently along faults or plates. The text supports this understanding because it describes the three types of faults and how they move and shift.

2. Example: *Plates* contributes to the description of earthquakes because it allows me to imagine how the parts of the Earth's surface fit together.

Sorting (page 85)

1. Example: I learned about different ways that you can sort rocks.

2. Example: The texts tells me that you can group things in different ways even though they might seem similar.

Transferring Energy (page 87)

1. The text tells the reader that energy can transfer when an object collides with another.

2. The effect was that the larger marble made the left marble travel farther.

Chemical Reactions (page 89)

1. The ingredients caused a chemical reaction, as evidenced by the change in temperature.

2. Examples include: the ingredients foamed and frothed, and the bottle felt warmer than the ingredients prior to mixing. Chemical reactions can cause materials to change form and can cause a change in temperature.

Creating Crystals (page 91)

1. Factors include: there may not have been enough sugar or salt added to the water, and the experimenter didn't use a measured amount but just added solids until he or she ran out. This may have affected the results because there were not enough dissolved solids in the water.

2. Experimental procedures could have been improved by using measured amounts of water and solids. He or she could also have measured the temperature where the bowls were kept. This could have affected the results because there were too many unknowns and the setting was not controlled.

Water Cycle (page 97)

1. Water in the ocean warms, it evaporates as water vapor, it rises to the sky, and it forms a cloud with more water vapor. It cools, grows heavy, and then falls as rain or snow. It flows down a river and joins the ocean again.

2. Evaporated water vapor forms a cloud. Clouds are part of the water cycle.

Answer Key (cont.)

Cloud Formation (page 99)

1. Example: This text is organized as a series of events, or a sequence text structure. I know because it explains how clouds are formed in order from beginning to end.

2. The text structure and author's purpose help a reader understand the process and order in which clouds are formed.

Precipitation (page 101)

1. The first paragraph describes what happens to water vapor in the atmosphere and as it falls to Earth's surface as precipitation. The second paragraph describes what happens when precipitation doesn't hit Earth's surface.

2. Example: This compare-and-contrast text structure is a good way to explain precipitation because it allows the author to discuss several types of precipitation.

Mohammed Karaji—Discovering Groundwater (page 103)

1. The text was a descriptive text structure. Each paragraph gives the main idea and details about part of Karaji's life and work. The first paragraph describes why his book was important, the second paragraph explains how his work progressed during his lifetime, and the third and fourth paragraphs describe the significance of his work.

2. The structure of the second paragraph is sequential. The signal words include: *so he wrote, when he was much older*, and *so he decided*.

The Desert (page 109)

1. The text says that the weather in the desert is very dry and that it does not rain much.

2. Example: The fact that best tell about the desert is that is very dry.

Tundra (page 111)

1. Sentences include: strong, cold winds sweep across the tundra; the top layer of the soil freezes in winter; and this soil is frozen all year round.

2. The text describes how the permafrost has retreated 50 miles north in the past 100 years as evidence of global warming.

Grasslands (page 113)

1. The text says that it does not rain often in grasslands. It also describes how fires can be started by a lightning strike that quickly spreads across the land.

2. The text says that fires clear the area and release minerals back to the soil.

Water Biomes (page 115)

1. Reasons include: many animals need freshwater to live, but only three percent of Earth's water is fresh; riparian biomes have running freshwater and support a variety of wildlife; they can store water and stop floods; and some animals live only in these biomes.

2. The author included it to illustrate people's impact on the land and the biome. It adds value because it allows the reader to get a sense of the impact humans may have on plants and animals.

The Beating Heart (page 121)

1. Example: The heart might be stronger at the end of some exercise.

2. Example: You could test how healthy people's hearts are who exercise against people who do not exercise.

Digestive System (page 123)

1. If the digestive system weren't working well, you could become very sick. The text states this in the first paragraph.

2. The mouth softens the food, the gastrointestinal tract makes the food parts smaller so the body can take out the nutrients before the remainder is eliminated as waste.

Skeletal and Muscular Systems (page 125)

1. The muscular system allows the skeletal system to move while the skeletal system gives structure to the body and to the muscular system.

2. Example: I notice that all the parts of the body work together. One system cannot exist without the other supporting it.

Answer Key (cont.)

Nervous System (page 127)

1. The brain is one part of the nervous system. It sends, receives, and interprets information from all the other parts of the body. Then, it sends messages to the body through the nervous system to control voluntary and involuntary activities.

2. Both voluntary and involuntary activities are controlled by the brain. Voluntary activities are conscious activities, while involuntary activities are the ones that happen in the background, such as breathing and digestion.

Outer Planets (page 133)

1. Both texts talk about planets in the solar system.

2. The first text talks about Uranus and how it ended up on its side. The second text talks about Neptune and the weather on that planet.

Comparing the Inner Planets (page 135)

1. Both texts are descriptive and give facts about planets in our solar system. They are different because one describes Mercury, and the other describes Venus.

2. Example: The scientific concepts are connected because both planets are close to the sun, have high temperatures, and spin slower than Earth.

The Depths of Space (page 137)

1. The first text describes how scientists believe the universe was created by the Big Bang. The second text describes the dangers of space and how astronauts protect themselves from space.

2. Some details include: how the universe is believed to have been created, how it started small but grew bigger, and how some scientists believe that it may start contracting again.

Space Exploration (page 139)

1. Both texts include details about space travel. The first text gives details about the first space pilot, NASA, and the space shuttle. The second text describes why humans began exploring space and the impact space travel has had on people and the planet.

2. Example: I think the second text better supports my understanding of space travel because it gives more details about the history of space travel.

Energy (page 145)

1. Example: It makes me think that all energy comes from the sun.

2. The author discusses the sun to explain where plants and people get their energy.

Potential Energy (page 147)

1. Example: If a dam broke, the water would begin moving like the ball in the text. It would release the potential energy of the water.

2. The author includes information about molecules because they have potential energy just like the dam and the ball.

Heat (page 149)

1. Example: The atoms in a bowl of hot soup are moving around very quickly. The hotter the soup, the faster the atoms are moving.

2. Example: If the atoms in the bowl of soup slowed down, then the soup wouldn't have as much energy, and the soup would be cooler. The text supports this because it says, "Atoms in cold things vibrate slowly. The atoms in hot things move around very quickly."

Solar Energy (page 151)

1. Example: *Solar* means energy that comes from the sun. Evidence that supports this is that all three of the first paragraphs describe energy from the sun, and the fourth paragraph says, "Even the car you ride in uses solar energy." The paragraph then describes how the fuel was created from the sun's energy millions of years ago.

2. Example: If the sun produced fewer photons, then there wouldn't be as much heat, light, or energy on Earth. This would mean that there would be less wind, water vapor, and clouds.

Notes

Notes